T0354471

Adventures of Mustang Sally

Adventures of Mustang Sally

A Memoir as told to Don Rashke

Mustang Sally and Don Rashke

authorHOUSE®

AuthorHouse™
1663 Liberty Drive
Bloomington, IN 47403
www.authorhouse.com
Phone: 1 (800) 839-8640

Published by AuthorHouse 05/01/2015

ISBN: 978-1-4969-7240-8 (sc)
ISBN: 978-1-4969-7241-5 (hc)
ISBN: 978-1-4969-7239-2 (e)

Library of Congress Control Number: 2015903867

Print information available on the last page.

This book is printed on acid-free paper.

Photo Credits: James D. Bass

Le' Image / Glamour Pets, photographer of front cover photo.

This book is dedicated to the loves of my life:
My beautiful and beloved wife Patricia
My six children: Guy, Sandi, Terri, Bruce, Richard and Dan
My adopted daughter Misti
They are all animal lovers.

Don Rashke

This book is dedicated to:
My Pals and my Pups, who have made me so happy

Mustang Sally

1

Where I Come From and How I Got Here

My name is Mustang Sally and I'm a Staffordshire Bull Terrier. I live in Texas now, but I was born in England. It's sometimes called Great Britain, but that includes England, Scotland and Wales. If you add Northern Ireland to the mix, it's called the United Kingdom or the UK for short. I hope that's not too confusing. When I was just a pup, I came to America and I've lived here ever since.

The history of my breed goes back a long way, all the way to the fifteenth century. I'm not very proud of some of it. Back then, what are called "blood sports" were common. These sports—if you can call them that—included bull and bear baiting and cock fighting. For example, when bulls were brought to market, dogs were allowed to attack them. This was a way of making the bulls' meat more tender. And the people who came to the market liked to watch. In fact, back then, we dogs had to fight with bears, bulls and other animals to entertain both royalty and commoners.

The hunters of the day, however, were more interested in work than entertainment. They were looking for a dog with the courage of a bulldog and the speed and stick-to-it-ness of a terrier. They tried breeding an English Bull Dog with a Manchester Terrier. The dog they got was called a Bull and Terrier. Well, duh! I can tell you, those early Bull and Terriers weren't bred to be pets. They had a job to do—and it wasn't pretty. This new breed, which weighed about ninety pounds, was very good at hunting bears. Big, black and brown, one-thousand-pound bears. Hunters would send three or four of my ancestors out to find a bear and attack it from different sides. And even though the bear had big sharp claws and teeth, those dogs were fearless. They would jump up and grab the bear with their strong jaws and attack its head and neck. And they just wouldn't let go. When the hunters heard all the growling and barking, they'd come up and finish off the bear with their guns. Of course, some of my ancestors got killed in these bear fights, and others got hurt real bad. But the hunters would take their hurt dogs home and nurse them back to health.

These hunters were so proud of their dogs that they named them after their village, Staffordshire, and added the two sides of the breeding to the name. So, we finally became the Staffordshire Bull Terrier—Staffie for short. I think that's a lot nicer name.

As time went by, our owners started using us for something else besides hunting bears. I guess it was supposed to be another kind of "entertainment," but it was horrible. I get very sad just thinking about it. Our breed was so strong and tenacious that these owners wanted to prove who had the best and fastest and strongest dog. So they made us fight each other! It was "kill or be killed" for us Staffies. We would fight until one of us was either dead or too hurt to stand up.

I don't know how anyone could enjoy watching that, much less bet on which dog would win. Finally, some people who loved animals started to complain about this cruel "sport." They forced the British Parliament to pass a law banning dog fighting. During all this time that the dog fighting was going on, these owners were breeding us Staffies for more speed and quickness. So, over time, we got smaller (and faster), but we still had lots of muscle.

About two hundred years ago, the UK had a terrible rat problem and many people got real sick. It was called a plague. It was so bad—especially in London—that hundreds of people died every month. There wasn't any medicine to cure the people in those old days. What they had to do was figure out how to get rid of the rats. Finally, they decided to use some of us "terrier" breeds to crawl down into the sewers and the holes where the rats hung out.

Terriers like the "Rat Terrier" and my breed, the "Staffordshire Bull Terrier" and others were let lose to go after those rats and kill them. My Staffie ancestors were really good at this job because of their big, strong jaws. Remember how they could take down those huge bears? Well, they could also grab a rat and kill it with one great big shake of their head. So all these terriers helped end the rat problem in England.

Finally, in 1935, The Kennel Club of Great Britain decided to recognize the Staffordshire Bull Terrier as a domestic breed. That meant Staffies could now be entered in "agility and conformation competitions." In other words—Dog Shows!

By this time, people had finally figured out that we Staffies were great companions. Over the years we just naturally learned to love our human "pals." And the humans saw that we were very good at protecting babies too—both our own dog babies and human ones. In fact, in England to this very day, we are known as "nanny" dogs because we're so patient and we can put up with a lot of pain. So the little ones—humans or dogs—can do almost anything to us (pinch, scratch, whatever) and we Staffies will always be gentle with them. And when we need a little break, we just walk away.

So after all these years, we Staffies are admired for our loyalty. That sure turned out to be the case with me. Over the years, I've had a very busy life. But the best part has been living with the family that I love. That's why I call my owners Pals. Now that I'm getting up in years, I'm thinking it's a good time to tell the story of my life so far. It starts with how I came to America.

I WAS BORN ON SEPTEMBER 14, 2003, in what is known as the "back country" in the Staffordshire region of England. How I got to America is pretty interesting, at least to me. Of course, as a pup I didn't know any of this. But I've heard the story many times whenever someone asks my Pals how they got me. So I can repeat it with my eyes closed.

It all started in November 2003 when my pals-to-be—Don and Patricia—went to visit Patricia's daughter Misti, who lived way up north in a place called Michigan. That's a long way from Texas where I live now, and even farther from England.

Here's how the story goes. Before my Pals get to Misti's house, Don says to Patricia: "She has a dog and I don't want anything to do with it!" Of course, as soon as Don comes in and sits down, this dog Megan jumps up and sits right in his lap. And every time my Pals and Misti come back from some outing, Megan waits for Don to sit down and then she jumps in his lap to cuddle.

So now Don is having second thoughts about dogs. He asks Patricia if maybe *she* would want a dog like Megan, who is a Staffordshire Bull Terrier. Then Don talks to Robert, Misti's neighbor, who explains why he helped Misti pick out a Staffie. It turns out that Robert is an expert show dog handler. He had dogs since he was a kid. He had studied their traits and he knew a lot. So Don asks Robert if he can find a nice female Staffie like Megan for him and Patricia. They want a girl dog because everyone says we girls are more gentle and we care more for our Pals. They say boy dogs only care about getting enough to eat.

Robert talks first to Megan's breeder, who says he doesn't have any pups right now. He says they should check with a breeder named Harry Doughty, who lives in England. Robert tells Don that he'll try to contact this Mr. Doughty the next time he's planning a trip to the UK.

"But you know these English breeders," he tells my Pal. "They don't like shipping any of their dogs to the U.S. unless they're sure they will be well cared for. But I'll see what I can do."

So Don and Patricia go back home to Texas and wait to hear from Robert. He doesn't call and they forget about dogs because they are very busy with other things.

OF COURSE, I DON'T KNOW ANYTHING about all these plans to get me to America. I'm just a two-month-old pup on the other side of the "Pond." All I know is my mom and my brother and four sisters and all the fun we're having playing with each other. One day a man comes to the kennel and starts looking at me and talking to Mr. Doughty. I don't think much about it at first, but after a few days the man comes back and they pack me up in a box called a "carrier" and away I go with this stranger.

I am *so* scared. All I know is that I'm alone with this strange man and I can't see my mom and the pups anywhere. The man isn't mean to me or anything. In fact, he has a nice voice and all the time he's driving he keeps saying things like "It'll be okay. Don't worry. We're going to Heathrow Airport." But I don't understand what any of this means. I just feel lost and alone.

When we finally get to this airport place, the man puts me in another kind of carrier. Then he carries me up some steps and into this long room with lots of seats all crowded together. The man holds the carrier (with me in it) on his lap and keeps talking to me in a quiet voice.

"You're pretty lucky to be in this puppy carriage," he says. "The airlines only let very small animals like you travel in these carriages. If you were even a little bigger, you would be in the hold." Of course, I have no idea what this "hold" is. But it sounds pretty scary to me. I would find out much more about "the hold" later in my life.

Sitting in my carrier on this strange man's lap, I'm just starting to calm down a little. Then a loud noise starts and I can feel this long room that we're in starting to move. Then it's moving faster and faster and all of a sudden we tilt back for a while. Then everything gets straight again. There's a little window next to our seat but all I can see is the blue sky and some clouds. So I have this feeling that we aren't in England any more. We stay on this plane (that's what it's called, I learn later) for what seems like hours and hours. Finally, the plane feels like it's slowing down. Then we have a few bumps and I think we're on the ground again. The man says to me: "We're here." I don't know where "here" is, but I find out soon enough.

The man carries me off the plane and we go to his house. Then a woman comes over and starts petting me and talking to me. This is when I first learn that the man is called Robert and the woman is called Misti. This Misti person talks to Robert for a while. But all the time she's also gently scratching me around my ears and rubbing my head and back. Oh that feels good! Then she puts on her coat. All of a sudden, she bends down, scoops me up in her arms, and wraps her coat around me.

"We don't have far to go," she says to me. "But I don't want you to get cold."

We go out the door and she carries me to another house not too far away. We go inside and this Misti puts me down on the floor and whistles. And what do you know—here comes this girl dog and she's a Staffie. Just like me! Misti tells me her name is Megan.

Right away I start to feel better. Megan is real friendly and she makes me feel right at home. So now I don't think so much about my brother and sisters and mom back in the UK. I start to settle down with my new family. Misti feeds me really good puppy food. And Megan and I go for walks together. She even lets me snuggle with her at night. I like my new home a lot.

One day a few weeks later, Misti starts putting things in a big box she calls a "suitcase." Then she gets Megan and puts her leash on. I think we're all going for a walk. But I'm wrong. Misti says she's taking Megan over to Robert's house to stay for a while. When Misti gets back she puts me in my carrier. Then she takes me and the suitcase out to her car. We drive for a while and then we stop and get out. I can see we're at one of those airports again. When we get on a plane, Misti keeps telling me I'm going to be a wonderful Christmas surprise for my new mom and dad. But I don't understand her and I'm scared again. Here I've been thinking I have a nice home and now she's taking me to another strange place. Who knows what I'll find there.

At least this plane ride is much shorter than the last one. Pretty soon Misti says we're about to land in Houston. Of course, I don't know what this Houston is or even that it's in Texas, if you can believe that. I'm just learning to be an American in Michigan. Now I'll have to start all over.

Misti carries me off the plane in my carrier. She says we're going to pick up our luggage. That's when I see—for the very first time— the people who are going to be my Pals. Of course, I don't know they're going to be my Pals. There is this very tall man and this pretty woman with blond hair. And it sounds like they didn't know I was coming. "What a surprise!" the pretty woman keeps saying to Misti. But soon they are talking to me too and they sound happy. Then we are walking out of the airport. It feels a lot warmer here. We all get in a car. These new people keep telling me I will love my new home. Then they start talking about what a wonderful "holiday" we'll all have. What's a holiday?

We drive for a while and then the car stops at this grand house. Misti takes me out of my carrier, puts my leash on and takes me around the house to this big backyard. These new people say it's for me to play in. Then they take me inside the house and feed me the same yummy food that Misti gave me back in Michigan. And now I learn what a holiday is. It's my first Christmas and I get lots and lots of toys. I'm also starting to explore this big house. After a few days,

Misti picks me up and puts me in her lap. She scratches behind my ears. Then she leans over and gives me a kiss.

"I have to go back to Michigan now," she says. "But I promise to come and visit you."

Then Misti and my new Pals say they're going to the airport. I'm sad after they leave. I miss Misti. I sure hope my new Pals come back. I like them and I think I'm going to like it here in Texas.

2

Lone Star Love

Once my new Pals, Don and Patricia, get over the surprise of my arrival, they start talking about what my "everyday" name should be. Listening to them talk, I learn that my official, "registered" name is Maktoum Hathrah. Even a pup like me is pretty impressed by that. It turns out that "Maktoum" is a Staffordshire Bull Terrier bloodline. It goes all the way back to my great, great grandparents on both my father's and my mother's sides of our family.

I also learn that my father is called the "sire" and my mother is called the "dam." And me, because I'm a girl dog, I'm called a "bitch." I don't like that very much. (Boy dogs are just called "dogs"—as if they run the whole show.) But I don't have any say in the matter. My official color is "Red and White." They also call me "pretty with permanent make-up." I figure out that all this fancy talk just means I have a nice, short, reddish-brown coat with some white markings and some pretty sexy black markings around my face and muzzle.

But back to the "name game." My new Pals decide that since their new baby (me!) is going to live in Texas, she should have a real Texan name. They start talking about how, a few years ago, they spent time on the Sixth Avenue "drag" in Austin. And how, in one of the clubs, they danced to the song "Mustang Sally." So that's it. I become Mustang Sally, or just Sally to my friends.

Now that the holidays are over, I seriously start to check out my new neighborhood. Everyone knows how curious puppies are. We just can't help it. Every day is a new adventure. One of the first things I do is take a look at the fence around my new backyard. My Pals don't realize that it isn't "puppy proof," but I sure do. In fact, I sneak out several times. One time I run after two dogs who are walking down the road with their "Master." I'm too young to know that you have to be careful which dogs you try to play with. But I sure learn my lesson quick. Before I know it, the bigger dog is grabbing my head. I start squealing. He lets go and, boy, do I run. I can hear my new Pal Don calling me and I can't wait to get back to him.

This experience teaches my Pal a lesson. He ties this stuff called "wire mesh" all the way around the bottom of our fence. I try to find some holes in it so I can get out and explore and have some fun. I mean, after all, I am a Terrier and it's bred into me to dig, tunnel and chase after things like balls and sticks. And squirrels. Don't even get me started on squirrels. I quiver. I *love* chasing squirrels. I think it's the most fun a puppy can have.

One day I'm playing in the backyard and this brownish, grayish "thing" comes flying over the fence. I don't know what it is, but I know I don't want it in my backyard. So I run after this thing. You have no idea how fast I am. I hear my Pals telling people all the time that I can do one hundred feet in three seconds, whatever that means.

Now I'm running after the thing so fast I can't stop. Nobody has told me about water or that there is a lake out here. Before I know it, I'm flying into this wet stuff and it is *cold*. I'll tell you, it really wakes me up. I can feel myself start to go under the wet and I can't get any air. As I sink down, I'm thinking I'm a "goner." But I start paddling my front legs and my head comes out of the water. And then I sink again. And then I paddle some more. Each time my head comes out of the water, I bark as loud as I can. Lucky for me, my Pal Don is in the backyard. My barking gets his attention real quick because I don't usually bark. He comes running over to the edge of the lake and keeps saying something that sounds like "holy shit." Then he lies down at the edge of the water and stretches out his arm. He grabs my neck and pulls me out. Just in time too.

I can't stop shaking and shivering. My Pal carries me into the house and wraps me in towels to dry me off and keep me warm. I think this is the first time I understand that my new Pals really care about me. And I've learned a lesson.

Now, whenever I hunt for squirrels, I always start my hunt down at the edge of the lake. That way, if I spot a squirrel, he'll be somewhere between the lake and the house. So when I go after him, I'll always be chasing him toward the house and I won't fall in the water.

One day, my Pals are outside watching me. They see me taking my "stalking stance," so they know I've spotted some kind of critter. Then I hear my Pal Don say to Patricia, "You know, Sally is really smart. She's going to run from the lake to the house so she won't overrun into the water again!" Hearing this makes me feel good. Even though I'm only seven months old now, I can figure out that if my Pals think I'm smart, they'll want to keep me.

Me at six months in my new backyard. Patricia picked out my stylish coat.

I'm happy because I like it much better here in Texas than in the UK. And now, I'm even catching on to how these "adults" talk. They have a whole different way of talking that's pretty cool. I've figured out some of it, but I wish I could understand more. They seem to like talking, except when they're "hollerin" at each other. Sometimes they talk really fast and I get so tired trying to understand them. After a while, I just go to sleep.

One of my Pals' expressions that I learn to understand real quick is: "Let's go bye-bye!" That means I get to ride in the car and see all kinds of new stuff. I never know what it will be. Going bye-bye is good because if I'm cooped up in the house too long, I get bored. And, believe me, that usually means trouble. When I get bored, I start looking for something interesting to do, like chewing on stuff. Boy, that gets my Pals really mad. After a few times getting wacked with a rolled up newspaper, I stop the chewing. I also discover a very soft, warm thing in one of the rooms. My Pals call it "the white sofa." I call it a nice bed. It's also the best place for looking out the window. What I really like is watching other dogs go by. Some of them are very funny looking. Their hair is so long that I wonder how they can ever stay clean.

I have to keep an eye out because my Pal Patricia goes crazy if she finds me on the white sofa. One time I'm on the sofa napping. She comes after me so fast that she scares the "living lights" out of me. I jump off that white sofa as quick as I can but, uh oh, on the way down I smash some big old pot she really likes. That's when I think she's going to kill me. But then my Pal Don comes to the rescue. He says to Patricia: "Look, she's only a puppy. You have to train her not to get on your precious stuff."

I may knock things over sometimes, but at least I'm not like those dogs I watch through the window. I've got nice short hair. My Pals tell everyone I'm really easy to care for. In fact, my Pal Patricia takes me in the shower with her to get nice and clean. That makes a lot of sense because we're both bitches. Whoops! I know you're not supposed to call girl pals "bitches," but one time I heard Don call someone a bitch. I hope he wasn't talking about Patricia because she's like a mother to me. They say I'm supposed to be "Don's dog," and he never hollers or hits me or anything. But I love both my Pals. And I guess Patricia's the one who has to make sure everyone behaves. I think this kind of person is called an "enforcer."

The other thing I really like besides going bye-bye and chasing squirrels and looking out the window is going for a walk with my Pals. I like seeing the other dogs in the neighborhood close up. Some of them are really weird looking. How can they see with all that hair in their eyes? Another one is big and black. One day when we're out walking, my Pals start talking to the black dog's Pal. He says his dog is a "Lab," whatever that means. All I know is that this is one fat dog. He waddles when he walks and his belly swings from side to side. I never want to get fat like that. I wouldn't be able to chase squirrels or have any fun.

EVEN THOUGH I REALLY LIKE OUR HOUSE on the lake, my Pals decide to move to an even bigger house. At least it's close, so it doesn't take us long to move there. My new home has so many rooms that it takes me a long time to explore them all. At least now I have lots of places to hide out if I get in trouble. One time, I'm checking out the rooms way at the top of the house. All of a sudden, I really have to go—you know, pee. Usually, I just "chirp" and someone comes and lets me out. (We Staffies don't usually bark, we make a kind of chirping sound like "eiha, eiha.") I'm chirping away but no one comes. So all I can do is go into one of the rooms and pee.

Not a good idea, I'll tell you. Boy oh boy, did I get it! Did you ever have your nose pushed into your own pee? Well, don't ever let that happen. It's bad.

I learned my lesson really quick. Now, when I have to pee, I just go and stand near a door that goes outside. When my Pals see me there they ask: Do you want to go potty? I could say: Of course, you idiot, why do you think I'm standing by the door! But that would really hurt their feelings. So I just wag my tail and they let me out.

Speaking of outside, I've found a way to squeeze through the fence here at my new house. One time I sneak out and just run and run until I run right up to this man and lady. We Staffies are so friendly that we'll go up to perfect strangers just to get petted. And if you don't pet us right away, we'll keep jumping on you until you do. So that's what I did and this man just picks me up, looks at my collar, and carries me all the way back home. I can tell that my Pals are shocked when the man knocks on the door and hands me over to Don. They didn't even know I was gone. But they don't bawl me out because they're just happy I'm back. Later I hear them say it's lucky I wasn't hit by a car. I don't really understand that because I like cars. I go bye-bye in the car and I don't think it would ever hurt me.

After that adventure, my Pals have a man come over to the house and put some extra stuff in the fence so I can't squeeze through anymore—just like they did at the other house. Fixing the fence takes a while, so every time they let me out to do "my business," one of my

Pals comes along so I don't "get into trouble." I can't figure out what they mean because I'm just having fun.

ONCE I GET A LITTLE OLDER, my Pals start taking me to a place they call the "puppy park." There are all kinds of dogs there, but no puppies. And there aren't any dogs like me either. Back in England, there are lots of Staffies, so you're always running into some of your "relatives." It's like a small town. You know everyone. But they don't have a lot of room over there in England. Here in Texas, everything is BIG. Or so they say. I can't speak for the whole state, but I do know we have big trees and big houses here. And a big puppy park.

I'm scared the first time we go to the park. But most of the dogs and some of the bitches are pretty nice. After a while, I just start running all over the place and say hi to everyone. This doesn't sit so well with my Pal Patricia. She says I'm stirring everyone up. But all we dogs are doing is chasing each other around. At one point, I have four dogs trying to catch me. No way that is ever going to happen. I can beat any dog, except maybe the skinny one with the long legs. I can tell you, when that dog stretches out, it's like he saying to everyone: I'm outta here.

After a while, I get pretty hot so I look for a shady spot under a tree or a bench. Finally, one of my Pals figures out that I need some water. It's not that they're dumb or anything. They just have a lot to learn. And so do I.

3

Show Time

Now that I'm almost two years old, I'm happy to be settled down with my Pals in our new home. But I think they've got other ideas. One day they decide to drive down to a place called San Antonio to see a dog show. They don't take me, but when they get back, I listen to them talk. As I understand it, at the show Patricia sits down at the judges' table and starts talking with one of the judges. His name is Roger Pugh. And, would you believe it, he's from a town in Staffordshire, England. The same as me!

My Pals talk to this judge for a while and tell him they have an English Staffie. He gives them his card and says "stay in touch." When he gets back to England, he does some research. He writes to my Pals and tells them that he can trace my heritage back to South Africa. Wow! I wonder where that is. About a month later, my Pal Don gets this piece of paper from Roger in the mail. It's called a "pedigree" and it shows five generations of my ancestors. My "Maktoum" name turns up on both my father's and mother's side of my pedigree. I think that must be a good thing because Don makes a big deal of it.

Don is going to call Roger, but he has to wait until tomorrow because Texas and England have different times. It's much later there, I think. When Don finally talks to Roger, he learns that my Maktoum relatives were named after a Middle Eastern sheik who owns all kinds of animals—horses, dogs, camels. He must be very rich to have all those pets.

Roger is all excited about my family's breeding. He calls it "line breeding." My Pal Don seems excited too. It turns out that Don knows all about this line breeding stuff. I hear him tell Roger that when he was younger, he had a dairy farm in Wisconsin, and he used line breeding for his cows. After he talks to Roger, Don explains it all to Patricia and me. He says line breeding is skipping a generation. It might mean breeding a grandfather to a granddaughter. Or breeding the daughter of a mother's first litter (by one sire) to the mother's son by another sire in another litter. In that case, my Pal tells us, the female would be bred to her half-brother. If line breeding is done carefully, Don says, it will preserve the best traits of a bloodline.

All this mixed up breeding stuff goes right over my head. But everyone else seems pretty excited. Then they start talking about me. Now my ears really perk up! Like they do every time I hear my name. Or when I hear someone coming to the door. My Pals say my ears are my "antennas."

Later on, this judge Roger Pugh writes to us on his computer. It's like magic. My Pals and Roger can write back and forth to each other so quick even though he's in England and we're in Texas. It's almost like talking. Roger tells my Pals that they should have me tested for any eye problems or other things. This will go on my "record" so I have a history, especially for breeding. Roger tells Don that this testing is done at some dog shows. He says Don should check with the AKC (that's the American Kennel Club) to find out which ones do it. So here they are talking about this "breeding" thing again. I don't understand, but I guess I'll learn soon enough.

I CAN USUALLY TELL which day of the week it is by the way my Pals act and what happens at our house. When the cleaning lady comes, it must be Wednesday, and when they get certain deliveries, it's Monday or Thursday. I know when it's Saturday because we go bye-bye a lot to run errands and have fun.

First thing on Saturday, we usually go to the grocery store. I can tell because a lot of the stuff my Pals bring back to the car smells so good. Then we go to a place called The Cleaners and my Pals pick up clothes that are all wrapped up but you can see what's inside. But the best place we go is called McDonald's where we all get hamburgers. Of course, that means I'm not so hungry at dinnertime. My Pal

Patricia doesn't like that. But what does she expect. I'm still a puppy and my stomach's not that big.

Today is Saturday but we're not running errands. My Pals say we're going to a dog show in Navosta, Texas. We don't have to drive very long to get to this Navosta place. Now Don says we need to look out for the Grimes County Fair Grounds. In no time we're there and let me tell you something. This dog show is really big. It seems like there are hundreds of dogs—all different kinds, I mean breeds. I look around as much as I can, but the first thing my Pals do is take me over to this doctor. He shines a light in my eyes and then sticks me with some needles to check for diseases, just like Mr. Roger said.

After the doctor thing is over, we walk around the show area and I start chirping because I'm so happy to see all these other dogs. Then this lady comes over and says her name is Grace. She asks my Pals if she can take a look at me. Then she says, "You have a beautiful Staffie here." This nice lady tells my Pals that she heard me chirping (like all us Staffies do) and she just followed the sound until she found me. I'm listening pretty carefully to all this, but my antennas really perk up when the lady asks my Pals if she can put a "lead" on me for a walk.

That's okay with everyone, including me, so Grace and I walk back and forth for a while. When that's over, Grace tells my Pals that I have natural ring ability and that they should consider training me for dog shows.

"This bitch has some really good qualities," Grace says. "Just look at that face!"

My Pal Don asks Grace how she knows all this. She says she's a Staffordshire breeder. In fact, she's showing one of her male dogs here using a handler. What's a handler? I wish I could ask. I guess I'll just have to keep my eyes open and my ears up and see if I can figure it out.

We all trot over to see Grace's dog. Turns out, he has just won "best in breed" at this show and will be in some kind of group judging later in the day. Patricia asks Grace what she would have to do to learn how to show me. My antennas go up again. The three of them talk for a while and decide to meet every Tuesday night for a couple of hours to train me.

Now this is a little tricky. I have to be careful what I say here because I don't want to upset anyone. But really! Train *me*? I know what to do. It's bred into me. This training will be for my Pals. They're the ones who need it.

THE NEXT TUESDAY NIGHT, we take off for Houston where we're going to meet Grace at some dog training place. Houston is a big city, not like Montgomery where we live. I know because I've gone "bye-bye" there to see Patricia's daughter Misti. Remember her? She's the one who first took care of me in Michigan. Misti lives in Houston now. And she's also Don's daughter because he "adopted" her. I guess that's kind of what he did to me.

It takes us a long time to get to Houston because there are so many cars on the road. And they go a lot faster than us. Finally we get to this building that's called "My Dog and Me." When we go inside there's a big hall and I can see twelve other dogs. I hear someone say that sometimes there are more than twenty dogs. We're all on our leashes and we take turns walking with our "handlers" over to a man who pretends to be the judge.

When it's our turn, Patricia and I walk over to the "judge." He tells us what we're doing wrong and what we should be doing. Because there are other dogs here with their people, we all catch on pretty quick. After about twelve walks back and forth, Patricia figures she's got the idea. And the judge agrees. He says: "Okay. Now just get in some shows."

When we get back home, Patricia decides she's ready to go to a real show and try to win. But my Pal Don doesn't know anything about showing dogs. He doesn't even know how to sign me up for a show. He has to ask Grace about everything. Grace says, "You just have to get online with Onofrio." Well, what the heck is Onofrio? Don is as clueless as me. Grace explains that Onofrio sponsors a bunch of dog shows around the country that are approved by the AKC. So each time you win at one of these Onofrio shows, you get points toward being a "champion." I guess that's important.

Grace can tell we're really confused. I mean, Don keeps asking her questions and I just stand here looking up at her. So finally, she writes everything down for us. It's pretty hard at first but little by little, we start to figure out this "show thing." Grace is such a nice, smart lady.

The first show we try out is in San Antonio. We know the way because my Pals went to a show there last year. It's where they met the English judge, Roger Pugh. He isn't here this time, but there sure are lots of dogs and people. I'm very confused, but my Pal Don knows what to do. He studied all the rules before we left home. He reads a lot and he seems to know everything. People ask Don stuff and he always has an answer. I wish I could read. I wouldn't even know how to get to San Antonio in the first place. But my Pal just looks at a big piece of paper called a map and drives us right here.

San Antonio is fun. We stay in a really nice place called "One of the Best Hotels." Most of the people there just love to ask my Pals if they can pet me, especially the kids. But some people are scared. They walk as far away from me as they can. I just don't understand that. Don't they know I would never hurt them?

At the show, when Patricia walks with me, the judge always says nice things. Whenever this happens, I always look right at the judge (sometimes it's a man, sometimes a lady) so they'll know that I agree with them. They always give Patricia a blue ribbon, so we must be doing something right. I find out later that the best ribbon to win is purple and yellow. That's for Best in Breed competition. That's what I want to win some day.

On the way home from San Antonio, my Pals say I won my first "major." Here's the way it works: Whenever there are a lot of dogs in a show they call it a "major" because it's much harder to win with all the competition. But that's just one of the rules they have. I don't understand who makes up all these rules, but they must be important. My Pal Don says everyone seems to know them and if you make a mistake, they are sure to correct you.

I think I'm going to like these dog shows. Everywhere we go they always have treats. And when I walk with Patricia around the ring, everyone claps and yells nice things. It makes me feel good that so many people like me. I just want to go and give them all a kiss. But they don't allow that. Besides, I've learned that not everyone likes to get licked on the face. At least that's one way I can tell which people are really dog lovers. They're the ones who don't mind when I lick their face.

On the way back home from San Antonio, we stop at a big open space. It's called a field. My Pal Don takes my leash off and says: "Now Sally, you have to behave and listen to me. OK?" Of course, I wag my tail and then go off for a romp in this nice field. When I get too far away, Don says: "Far enough." At first I don't understand. Then Don comes and gets me and we walk back to the spot where he said "far enough." And he says it again.

It doesn't take too long before I understand what he's trying to tell me. However, my Pal Patricia doesn't like this game at all. She says something is going to happen to me and we'll all feel bad. But my Pal Don is pretty stubborn. He takes me to a different place in the field and we practice this romping and "far enough" game until he's sure I know when to stop running so I don't get into trouble.

THE NEXT THING I KNOW, we're on our way to another dog show. I think it's a really big national show, because Patricia is very excited about it. This one is far away in a place called Perry, Georgia. It takes us a couple of days to get there. I don't mind because we stay in nice places called motels along the way where there's lots of room for me to romp. Of course, my Pals treat me pretty good too because they want me to be happy when we get to the dog show.

One time we stop where there's a big field with a very steep hill that goes straight down to the road. When Patricia finds Don and me out there, she is really upset. She's worried that I'll run down that hill and end up in the road and get hit by a car. Now I don't like it when my Pals argue because it makes me nervous. I come back and start circling around them. Finally, they notice me and stop arguing so I'll calm down. Then Don says to Patricia: "Look, I'll show you. Sally will *not* go into the road. We'll start up here and when she gets near the road I'll say, 'far enough.' You'll see how well she listens."

Of course I'm smart enough to listen to my Pal. As soon as Don says "far enough" and calls me, I come right back to him. I guess Patricia believes us now because she turns around and walks away.

This "far enough" business is sort of like going into a show ring. Before a show class starts, Patricia always takes me for a walk on my leash. We only go so far and then I can just feel she's about to stop. So I stop too. It's like a real small signal she's giving me that you can't even see. Then she'll start to turn and I turn too. It's like when you see two people out walking together. No one says anything, but they just know when to stop. It's the same with us dogs. At first, when we're young, we may get a little tangled up now and then. But after we practice our stopping and starting and turning with our handler, we almost always know just what to do—and when to do it. This is all practice for what I'll be doing in the ring. And at every show, Don also goes out with me and we practice "far enough" so there won't be any problems when I'm off my lead.

Finally, we get to Perry, Georgia. Wow, this is the Big Time! Don says the show is being held at the Georgia State Fair grounds. There are so many buildings and it seems like there are thousands of dogs. It's such a long way from the parking lot to the building that my Pals rent a motor cart to ride in and carry our supplies. I sit between them on the seat and off we go.

At first, all the buildings look the same to me. But pretty soon I know I'll be able to tell them apart. My nose is working all the time and each building smells different. Finally, we get to the building where we'll be showing. It's so big that I wonder how we'll ever find our show ring. But Don knows just what to do. He checks with a lady at the main desk and she tells him where our ring is.

My Pals set up their chairs near our show ring and Patricia takes me for a long walk around the fair grounds. She's "shopping," so I know I'll get something good. Patricia loves to shop. And she always remembers me. This time I get a new leather lead and a chew bone treat. Back at our chairs near the ring I sit with Don while Patricia goes around and talks to people. She makes friends real easy and remembers peoples' names even after we leave a place. In fact, her people memory is almost as good as my smell memory.

We win in Georgia, and everyone is so happy. I'm now called a "champion." One lady even comes over to Patricia and tells her what a good win this is for me. Turns out I even beat her bitch, who was "the best of opposite sex at Westminster." That Westminster thing must be really important because all these other people also come over and congratulate Patricia and pet me and say nice things. But what Patricia says to me after they are all gone is the nicest: "Sally, you are the best!"

4

Up North

Soon after the big Georgia show, it starts to get really hot in Texas. My Pals are talking about "going to Wisconsin." Of course, I know by now that my Pal Don is from that place, but I don't know where it is. My Pals keep talking about a "cabin" up there. They say it will be a great place for me to play outside and we can go down to the lake. This last part has me a little worried. I've had enough trouble with lakes.

My Pals load up the car the day before we're going to leave. Early in the morning we start off and drive and drive. I have never been so far away from my home, even when we went to Georgia. I'm sitting on the back seat and there are all kinds of things to look at through the windows. But after a while, I start to yawn and before I know it, I'm sound asleep. I only wake up when the car stops. Are we at Wisconsin yet? No such luck. Don has to get some gas for the car and Patricia takes me out to do my business. Then we eat some goodies that Patricia brought along and off we go again.

It's getting late now and we still haven't gotten to the hotel that they say "takes dogs." I don't like the sound of this because I always go where my Pals go. But the next thing I know, we are all in this hotel together. I guess my Pals decided not to put me in a hotel that just takes dogs.

Early the next morning, we're off again. But not until we all eat and my Pals have their coffee. Finally, in the afternoon, we reach this cabin they've been talking about. It looks pretty nice on the outside.

When we go in, I check everywhere just to make sure there are no other dogs. I don't mark anywhere, but I do want everyone to know who this place belongs to.

On my rounds I see a space way up at the top of the cabin. My Pals call it "the loft." I think this will be the best place for me to see what's going on. There is also another place down below. My Pals call it the "lower level." From there, a door leads straight out to the lake. My Pals say it's about one hundred feet down some steps. Patricia likes to walk down there, so I go with her. Don's not really up for all this climbing so he watches us from the back porch. My Pals call it "the veranda."

Let me tell you about this veranda. It's pretty neat. I can run back and forth across it and see through the posts that hold up the railing. There's only one problem. I can see squirrels through the posts, but I can't go after them. That, as my Pals say, really bugs me. I just sit and look through the posts and quiver all over until the squirrel decides he has tortured me enough and runs away.

There really are a lot more interesting things to see and chase up here in Wisconsin than in Texas. And now I even know what most of them are called. Every time I hear a sound I scamper out to the veranda and start making all kinds of noises. Then my Pals come out and describe what's going on. I see a lot of deer, which I think are very pretty. Regal is what my Pals call them. And boy, can they run and jump. I have never seen anything jump as high as a deer.

The "cabin" in Wisconsin

Then there are the foxes. They are so fast and they can slide in and out of briars and logs and they can hide in tree hollows. I know where they are, but I can't sit around and wait all day for them to come out. Of course, they're just waiting for me to turn my head for a second. And when I do, they sneak off. I guess that's where the word "foxy" comes from.

Today, a chipmunk runs across the veranda and I almost crash into the posts trying to catch it. But that darn thing goes right under the bottom railing. When it gets past me, it just stands up on its hind legs and stares at me. That makes me really mad, so I bark at it. A lot of good that does!

Some people don't believe that dogs talk, but let me tell you, we do. Especially Staffies. For example, that bark at the chipmunk says I'm pretty mad. And when someone scratches my head, I kind of moan, meaning I really like this. If I want to go someplace—like get out of the car—I'll chirp. In the show ring, chirping is the only sound I make, even though there are many other dogs around. But if I see dogs outside just walking around with their own pals, I'll bark. It's not a really loud bark, just enough to get their attention and say hi. Just like our pals, we dogs talk to each other all the time in our own way.

My body language is also a way of talking, and my Pals pick up on that very quickly. For example, if they try to give me a treat that I don't really like, I'll just look the other way. Then if they put it down on the floor, *maybe* I'll pick it up. But when I do, I'll swing my head away from them. They know I'll eat it, but I'm not happy with it. When I put my tail between my legs, you can be pretty sure I'm worried about something. If a growl goes along with that, you better be careful because I don't like what I see and I feel threatened. If, along with my tucked tail and growl, I bare my teeth, I'm about to attack. That doesn't happen very often.

My Pals bought a boat that they've tied up to their pier down at the lake. Now they're saying we can all go out on the water and fish and just cruise around in the sun. What are they thinking? I'm not going near that lake, not after falling in the water back in Texas. Guess what? It turns out I don't have much say in the matter. Before I know it, I'm being "helped" onto the boat.

With the motor running it's a little noisy out here on the water. I sit in the seat next to my Pal Don so that nothing bad will happen to me. It's getting pretty hot. Patricia brings out a jug of water, pours some in a dish for me, and sets it on the floor of the boat. So now I have another problem. I either have to get off my seat to get a drink or stay up here and die of thirst. Don's watching me all this time. Finally, he helps me down and I carefully slink over to the dish so I won't fall out of the boat.

I'm starting to enjoy this boat ride a little when the sound of dogs barking perks my ears up. It is torture to hear a bark and not know where it's coming from. I get up my courage and jump back up on the seat and carefully put my paws on the side of the boat. Sure enough, I can see a nice looking dog on the shore. I get a little excited and start wagging my tail. Patricia says, "Maybe she's coming into heat." I wonder what that means?

After a few times out on the lake, I'm getting used to these boat rides. I just don't like to jump from the pier onto the boat. Now, when we come back in, I even go off and investigate the shoreline. It's real different from the one in Texas. There's no way you would fall in over your head like I did back home. Here I can put my paw in the water to see how cold it is and how deep. Sometimes, I'll walk along the shore in a little bit of water and it doesn't even scare me.

There is a problem, however. While walking close to the shore, I sometimes get into mud. You don't know what "upset" is until you've seen Patricia react to a muddy Staffie. Being washed down with cold water from a hose is no fun, believe me. And she is relentless. The more I shake the water off, the more she sprays me. After this experience, I'm going to stay away from mud.

Now my Pals are starting to take me "fishing." That means a ride on the boat. Then they pull out this stick with a string on it and throw the string in the water. And sometimes, everyone gets excited and they pull the string out of the water and it has this thing flapping at the end of it. They call it a fish. So far, I haven't tried to grab one of these fish.

ONE DAY DON GOES OFF in the car and comes back with another guy. This stranger doesn't have to get very close before I smell *cats*. We dogs can always smell them. Now, I know some people say dogs and cats can live together and even be friends, but I don't believe it. Cats are our mortal enemies. They snarl and hiss and when you chase them they jump on you. They are as bad as squirrels.

This guy with the cat smells turns out to be Don's younger brother, Richard. He's nice enough but I think at first he's a little scared of me. I finally win him over and he starts to pet me, especially when we're out on the porch and Don is around. I think Richard is Don's best friend—after Patricia, of course. Don always listens very carefully when Richard is talking. That's really saying something because my Pal doesn't always listen to people. He pretends to, but I know better. I can always tell when he's just tuning them out.

In the evening, when we're all sitting out on the veranda, Patricia says, "Do you hear the loon?" We all stop and listen, including me, and before you can say "loon," another long, sweet sound comes over the lake and my antennas perk up. Patricia says there must be a pair of them out there. I don't understand how she knows this. Maybe it's just one loon making all these calls.

Sometimes it's hard to figure these humans out. Like when Richard and Patricia talk about going fishing. They never include Don, but he never talks about going either. Maybe it's too hard for him to get up early. Or maybe he just wants to let Richard run the show. So Richard says they should plan to get up early and go after some "bass." What's that? I thought they were going fishing. And does Richard know that Patricia hates getting up early? I watch them head down to the pier where Patricia starts up the motor on the boat for practice. I guess Richard doesn't know how to do that.

The next morning I'm very surprised when Patricia really does get up early. She even wakes me up. After letting me out for my business, she and Richard head down to the boat. I'm all by myself in the house now, except I know Don's sleeping in the bedroom. Smart guy. After a while, Don gets up and makes coffee. Then, as usual, we jump in the car and drive down to the gas station to get a newspaper. When we get back, Richard and Patricia come up from the lower level smiling and carrying a bucket. Richard says they caught the limit of bass and Patricia holds up a chain of wiggly things. Now I understand. Bass are fish! They take pictures of their "catch" and swear they will never tell anyone where their secret "fishing spot" is.

In the evening, Richard and Patricia cook up the fish. They smell really good and my mouth is watering. Then Patricia gives me a taste. Hey, they can go fishing anytime. And they do. And they always take pictures of themselves holding the "bass." And they tell everyone they

Patricia with her catch of bass.

talk to about how they've caught all these fish. I guess they must be proud because it looks pretty hard. I know I could never figure out how to do it. One morning I decide to get up early and go out fishing with them. After just a short time on the boat, I can tell they really know what they're doing.

"I've got one," Patricia says.

"Okay," Richard says and drops his stick.

"Get the net," Patricia says.

Richard grabs this bag filled with holes and dips it in the water and up it comes with a fish. Amazing! I think when humans fish it's like when we dogs play. We're all just having fun. The best part is that, after they have their fun, we all get to eat it.

You have to go fishing with them like I did to see how all this works. It will be worth it!

IN THE AFTERNOON, RICHARD SAYS he's going down to play his horn. I haven't heard of this kind of "play" before, but all of a sudden some sounds come up from the lower level. They sound pretty good. Almost like what you hear on TV. We watch TV every night, but not until everyone discusses what's on and agrees what to watch.

My Pal Don says Richard is very talented. He says Richard can even write music for a whole orchestra just by playing his saxophone—that's what his "horn" is called. I don't have a clue how he can do all this, so I just go and lie down by the fireplace and listen. I also like to listen to the loons late at night, especially when everyone else is sleeping. It's such a beautiful sound. It usually puts me to sleep too.

I CAN TELL SUMMER IS COMING TO AN END up here in Wisconsin because the leaves are starting to fall. There is still fishing, but my Pals are saying Richard has to leave pretty soon. After he goes, I know we'll be traveling soon too. My Pals start to bring out certain clothes and they're checking things all around the cabin. They empty ashes from the fireplace and put the lawn furniture away. Patricia has this nice lady come over and help clean the cabin. I like her, but when I jump up to get petted, I guess I scratch her. Maybe she needs to wear long pants like everyone else does around here.

Now that we're packed and ready to leave, I sure hope we're going home to Texas. It's nice to go away. But it's always better to come home.

5

Back in Texas, But Not for Long

Once we get home, my Pals start talking about getting a "handler" to show me now that I'm a "champion." I guess being a champion is a big deal because my Pals say now I have to compete with all the "specials." There are so many of these show terms that I can hardly keep track. We champions are called "specials," "champions," and "variety." If we aren't called one of those names, we are "class dogs." I guess class dogs just mean we are regular dogs. Notice they don't even mention bitches.

I may not know what all these terms mean but I can tell you one thing. When I go into the show ring, I know which dogs showing with me are the most handsome. Even though I'm paying attention to my handler, who's showing *me* off, I'm still checking out those dogs very carefully. I guess I'm pretty competitive because I want to get everyone's attention with my energy. And what's really fun is to meet up again with some of the same dogs and judges from other shows.

It's kind of cold now, even here in Texas. The show I'm going to in Houston is in an unheated barn, which I don't like at all. At least it's not outside on grass. That's the worst thing. Show grass is not at all like the grass at home. It feels funny to my feet. But this cold barn in Houston is bad enough.

Cold or not, I won't let it stop me. Sometimes I get mad because I think we bitches aren't valued as much as the male dogs. But it just makes me want to beat the boy dogs even more. And I do. In fact, I beat the number one Staffie "dog" twice this weekend with the Best in Breed selection. His "registered" name is Belnore Dream Keeper, but everyone calls him Beau. Then the next day he beats me and I get the Best of Opposite Sex selection. That's what they give us bitches when we come in second to a dog. When the dog comes in second to a bitch, they give him the Best of Opposite Sex selection too. Is this clear? I really think it would be easier just to call us Boy Dogs and Girl Dogs. Why do they have to make things so complicated?

I've barely finished my two wins at the Houston show when my Pals get a letter. It says that I'm invited to the Eukanuba National Dog Show in Palm Springs, California. Wow! This is pretty big stuff—or so they tell me. My Pals are really happy and now they're trying to figure out how we're all going to get there. Well, you know my Pal Don by now. It doesn't take him long to work everything out.

I hear Don ask Patricia if she would like to look at "motor homes." I can't believe what I'm hearing. People have so many places to have homes—in Texas, in Wisconsin, and now in a Motor. One afternoon, my Pals leave me at home and go off somewhere until dinnertime. About a week later, up comes this great big box on wheels and parks in front of our house.

Don says to me: "Come on, Sally, let's go for a ride in our new motor home." I'm not so sure about this, but I do go outside and look around. Man oh man, this thing is as big as a train car I saw once. Now Patricia's standing inside the door of the thing waving me toward her.

"Come on up, Sally," she says. I don't move an inch so she gets down and comes over to me.

"Here, I'll help you," she says.

"Really, you don't have to. I'll just stay right here." I wish Patricia could hear me. But she just scoops me up and before I know it, I'm inside this "motor home."

My Pals shut the door and I take a little peek around. The place has a nice carpet and Patricia's sitting on a bench against the wall. Way in the back there's a bed. It really is a home. While I'm walking around looking things over, Don makes some coffee in the little kitchen. I know it's coffee because it smells the same as when we're in our other homes. (Don't forget, we Staffies have very good noses.) I decide to go over and sit near Patricia's feet. I figure this is the best place for me. I know Don would never let Patricia get hurt, so I should be safe here. Meanwhile, Don has started this motor thing up and is driving around the neighborhood. From the inside it feels almost like a car—a very big car. I can see Don up front in the driver's seat, so I sneak up for a look-see. These are some big windows! I'm up high and I can see a whole lot more than in a regular car. Hey, maybe this isn't so bad after all!

Don does some more practice runs in the motor home. Then we pack up and we're off to the "Eukanuba" in California. Now, I don't know where or how far away this California place is, but it turns out to be pretty far. We have to make a lot of stops. What's really nice is that we get to sleep in the motor home. No more looking for hotels that take dogs. And we don't have to load and unload our suitcases. And all our food and treats are right here. Cool!

We finally get to this Eukanuba. It has the most dogs I've ever seen in one place. And there are so many different breeds here too. My Pals put me on a leash and we head out to see what this show is all about. First, we go into a great big room where they have all these tables. It seems like a thousand. And there are more show rings than I've ever seen. I don't know how we will ever know where to go, and when.

It's a good thing my Pal Patricia is smart. She gets something called a catalog that she says will help us. Sure enough, it tells us where we have to be and when we have to be there and who our competition will be and who the judges are. Now we don't have to worry. We can just go in there and win! The only problem is that tomorrow we have to be here at 9:00 a.m. That's pretty early for Patricia, so I expect to hear some complaining.

Well, we do get up early the next morning. Then, after we get all our business out of the way, we head over to the competition. There are buildings everywhere. It's quite a long walk to get to the building with the auditorium. But it's pretty out here and there are all kinds of smells for me to check out, so I don't mind the walk at all.

When we finally get to the right show ring, there are about twenty-five other Staffies in the ring. That's the most I have ever seen in one place, and they're looking pretty good. I know I will have to do my best or I'll be left behind. When it's all over, I don't win Best of Breed or even Best of Opposite Sex. But...I do get an "Award of Merit," so I won't have to go home with an empty paw. And my Pals and I are invited to a party this evening. It's the Staffie "Top Twenty Show." I'm thinking that must mean I'm in the top twenty of our breed. But my Pal Patricia says it's even better. I'm number seven in our breed. "Now that's really something," she tells Don. She says there are thousands of Staffies in the United States. Of course, not all of us compete in shows. But just the same, I think number seven is quite an honor!

I also think this "Top 20" show is really just an excuse for all the Staffie breeders to get together and check out their competition. But it must be pretty special because everyone is dressed up real fine. The judges are wearing what Patricia calls "tuxedos," and all the women are eyeing each other. I do this with other dogs too, especially the bitches I have to beat. The boy dogs here are pretty good looking, I must say.

We have a great time at the "Top 20" party. The next day I'm all ready for another competition, now that I know what I'm up against. But hey, it turns out all this travel is just for one show day. Still, as we're heading home, we're all pretty happy that we made the trip and found out that I'm pretty far up in the standings.

NOT TOO LONG AFTER WE SETTLE DOWN back home, Patricia starts dragging out all the "winter" things. This tells me Christmas must be coming up again. I'm sure of it when she starts putting together the Christmas tree. She makes it pretty clear that all of this "stuff" is off limits to me. So I just go over to the other side of the room and watch. It seems like a lot of trouble, but when Patricia gets all these shiny things—they're called ornaments—on the tree and adds the lights, it sure does look good. I'm not surprised because Patricia really runs this house and she always makes everything look nice.

My Pal Don thinks so too. He comes into the room and says: "Boy, that Christmas tree looks good." Then the next thing that comes out is a bunch of boxes covered with pretty paper and ribbon. Patricia puts them all around the tree. I'm sitting here wondering what will come next.

A couple of days later, I find out. All these people I don't even know come over to the house. I mean, there's a whole gang of them— grownups, kids of all sizes, and even babies. They're all having fun and opening the pretty boxes. Then they squeal when they pull out the stuff that's inside. Everyone seems to be having a great time. And I think everyone loves me, especially the kids. They take turns petting me and letting me sit in their laps. Then Patricia brings out all this good stuff to eat, and everyone gives me a little bite of something. As far as I'm concerned, this should happen every day. Christmas is the best!

Christmas is BIG at our house.

About a week later comes this other holiday called New Year's Eve. Of course, Patricia has to get me all dolled up in another outfit. And lots of people—but no kids that I can see—come over for drinks and food. After a while, they're all eating and drinking and talking and laughing and having such a good time that they don't even notice me.

This party just goes on and on. When I can't stand it anymore, I walk down the hall to my Pals' bedroom to take a little nap. I'm just dozing off when I hear all these voices yelling together: Five, four,

Patricia and me all dressed up for New Year's Eve.

three, two, one. Happy New Year! After a while, the voices get quieter and I'm asleep. I only wake up when Patricia comes to help me get out of my costume. I think New Year's Eve is over at last.

6

A Big Change and a Close Call

I'm three years old now. That means on the human calendar I'm twenty-one. All grown up. I've had what they call my first cycle. I hear my Pals talking about "getting me bred" on my next cycle. I don't know what this means so I listen up, as we Texans say. Don thinks maybe we should call Grace and ask if we can arrange for a breeding with her dog, Celebrity Ice Cube (better known as Mel). I think that's a good idea because, whatever they're talking about, Grace can explain everything.

I guess they figure out what to do because about ten days later they take me to meet a handler who is showing Grace's dog Mel. Don tells the handler that he has all the paperwork done. What's this "paperwork"?

Don says the plan is to try putting together the "good genes" that go back a long way in the pedigrees of both me and Mel. Then, in future breeding, another line can be brought in. I'm thinking all this has something to do with the "line breeding" thing I remember hearing my Pals talk about. But if you can figure it all out, you're smarter than me.

After a while, when the humans finish all their talking, I find myself for the first time inside a kennel next to this boy dog, Mel. He seems quite nice. I had no idea these big-time show dogs could be so friendly. In fact, Mel is a perfect gentleman and waits for me to say it's okay for us to get together. Mel and I spend the night in the kennel and then, much too quickly, I'm on my way home. I think this stinks.

I'm just getting to know this nice boy dog and we have to leave. But no one seems to pay any attention to how I feel.

Here in Texas, it's starting to get warm. My Pals are talking Wisconsin again. I wouldn't mind a little vacation. I'm feeling pretty tired most of the time now and I'm starting to get fat. I know something's going on.

THIS TIME, WHEN WE GET TO THE CABIN, my Pals fix up some special new places for me to hang out and sleep. I hear them talking about whether I'll be a good mother to my pups. So that's what it's all about. Puppies! But how can they even ask such a question? Of course I'll be the best mother ever!

One night I really don't feel good. I know Don's sleeping in the bedroom so I walk over and lie down near Patricia, who's asleep on the couch. I've never felt this bad in my whole life and I don't know what to do. Both my Pals are sleeping. Finally, Patricia hears me whimpering and comes over to me. I try to stand up but I can't. Patricia looks scared and goes to wake up Don. He comes out and tries to get me on my feet. No luck. I just can't do it. My Pals talk for a while and decide to set the alarm clock to wake them up early so they can take me to a vet up in some place called Minocqua.

In the morning I'm not feeling any better. Don carries me out to the motor home and we get on the road real early. It takes about an hour to get to the vet and he's not even open yet. Finally, he comes to the door and they carry me inside. The doc takes a look at me and then he says to my Pals, "I really don't know what the problem is." He suggests that they take me to another vet across town. Maybe he can figure it out. So off we go again. This new vet is a nice fellow, but he doesn't know what's wrong either. All he can say is, "It looks serious. If you want, I can send you to a "referral only" veterinary hospital. But it's pretty far away, in Appleton."

Of course, my Pals say "Yes, let's do it." It takes us about four hours to get there, but at least one of the doctors sees me right away. He takes me into an exam room and he's really checking me over. Then more people in white coats come in and do some other stuff to me. I'm very tired by now, so I don't remember much. My Pals tell me later that they had to wait two hours before the doctor came out to see them. He told them it was going to take some pretty drastic medicine to make me better.

My Pals come back to see me in the kennel area where I'm resting. I don't have enough strength to chirp or even whimper. I just stare at my Pals. Patricia looks like she's going to get sick too. She starts crying so hard that the doctor asks if he can get her anything. He says she should probably go outside and get some air. My Pal Don is stronger. He stays right here with me and asks the docs all kinds of questions. They tell him to come back after lunch. They'll know more then.

After my Pals leave, the docs do some more tests on me. When Don and Patricia come back, the docs say the blood tests show some kind of poison or virus going through my body. Then I hear my Pal Don say: "Well, we want you to do whatever you have to do to save Sally. But we also hope you can save her pups." The doctor tells them he wants to keep me overnight to do even more tests. And they're going to keep me in isolation so they can watch me closely. Don says, "Okay, we'll be back in the morning about ten o'clock because we're up in Rhinelander, four hours away."

My Pals come in to say goodbye and Patricia looks like she's going to cry again. She says I look so sad. Well, I am sad! It's just not fair for me to be in this strange place all by myself.

The next day, I'm in my kennel at the hospital with something hanging around my neck and some needles sticking out of my leg. I'm feeling very sad and lonely. Then I hear my Pals' voices and I'm not sad anymore. I'm really excited—well, as excited as I can be in my condition. I hope they can help me get rid of all this stuff that's sticking in me. And I want them to get me out of here. When my Pals come through the door, it looks like Patricia's going to cry again. Don just stands there staring at me. The vet lady says they can pet me. They tell me they'll come back after they've had lunch and a conference with the doctor.

I wait and wait. It's getting late and I'm a little worried. The doctors have already fed me dinner. But where are my Pals? Finally, Don and Patricia come in to say goodbye. They say they'll be back tomorrow. Don tells the doctor I'm looking so much better, and he's glad to see me standing up. The doc says, "Yes, that's a good sign. But we have a long way to go."

Well, it's true. I've had a close call. The doctors have a hard time making me better and saving my pups at the same time. But now I know my pups are still inside me and all I have to do is get them born. After five days and $4,500, I'm ready to go home.

I'M SO HAPPY WHEN WE GET BACK to the cabin. My Pal Don shows me where he has set up a nice quiet place for me to have my pups. He's put down some new bedding, which I check out after I rest a little. I rummage through all the shredded paper my Pals put down to see if there's anything under it. Nope. While I'm doing this, I hear Patricia say all this rooting around must be a sign I'm about ready to have my pups. And she's right. The next morning, I try very hard to deliver my babies, but it's just not working. So off we go to the vet in Rhinelander.

At the clinic, I hear my Pals talking with the vet. The doc is saying that the first pup trying to come out is stuck because its head is too big. He says, "We'll have to do a caesarean section." I wonder what *that* means? But before I can think about it very much, I'm out of it. I'm so groggy when I wake up that I hardly know where I am. Then I remember and I want to see my puppies. The babies are in a basket and my Pals load it and me into the car. Then—here's the best part—I get to crawl in and snuggle with my brand new pups.

Boy, are they hungry! I tell them, "Hey, take it easy, I was just cut around there." But at their age, they don't really listen. All they want to do is eat. That's okay. I'm just so glad to be here with my babies that I clench my jaws and bear the pain. But as we're all settling down, I realize something is wrong. One of my pups is missing. I *know* I had four.

When we get home and my three pups are sleeping, I start hunting all over the cabin for the fourth one. I even hunt for it when I go outside. At first, my Pal Don doesn't understand what I'm looking for. Then he gets it and I hear him say to Patricia: "Of course—she's looking for the fourth pup. We just have to keep telling her there are only three." But I know better.

I sneak under the porch and start digging in the dirt. I'm sure my fourth pup must have gone down here. Now I can't get back out because the dirt keeps falling over me. I can hear my Pals calling, "Sally, Sally." Patricia sounds really upset. She keeps telling Don to "do something." He says he's going to take the truck and go look for me. Then Patricia hears me whimpering from under the porch. Then I hear Don say, "Wow, what a relief."

Don gets a shovel and digs me out. My Pals are very gentle with me. They don't seem to know what to do about my missing pup.

"I don't know how in the world she knows she had four pups," I hear Don say. "She was totally under anesthesia, but she seems to think the one that died should be here. It's amazing."

So now I know what happened and I'm very sad. But I can't think about that for long because it's a big job handling the three babies who *are* here. It seems like they want to nurse all the time. After they nurse, they take a nap. Thank goodness. At least then I can get a little rest myself. The bed my Pals made for us is great. It has a ridge along the wall that my pups can fit right under. They feel nice and secure there and it keeps me from accidentally rolling on top of one of them.

Each day, my Pals come over to our bed. They pick the pups up and pet them so they get used to people and aren't afraid. Then my Pals weigh each pup to make sure they're all growing like they should. I can tell you, this bunch has no problems in the eating department!

Patricia in 2006 holding my first babies. From left:
Lucy, Mak, and Killian.

Now the big discussion is: What shall we name the little ones—two boys and a girl. My Pals are having a lot of fun coming up with names for "the babies," as they call them. Finally, they agree. One of my boys becomes Killian. He's named after a brave English warrior. I think that's pretty neat because it reminds me of the history of our breed. And the other boy is named after me, in a way. He's going to be called Mak. That's short for the "Maktoum" line in our family pedigree. Finally, my little girl will be called Lucy. Patricia is just in love with her.

Of course, like me, all my pups will also have one of those serious sounding, registered names. These official names are the ones that will be used if my Pals ever decide to show my pups when they get older or to breed them.

We stay here at the cabin until the leaves turn from green to red and yellow. I don't know how long that is in people time, but it's been wonderful. I'm happy that things have been quiet too. I've had enough excitement to last me a long time. Every day the pups are learning so many new things. They're like little sponges—you know, just soaking up everything about this big new world they're in. I do have to keep an eye on them though. They don't have much experience and they're likely to get in trouble because they're so curious. I can't blame them. I think they get it from me. Remember some of my adventures when I was younger?

As the summer comes to an end, my Pals get ready for the trip back to Texas. Of course, the pups haven't a clue. All they know is the cabin. Boy have they got a surprise coming! We finally get the motor home loaded up and head south. Each time we stop for a break, Don puts up this portable "corral" he bought for the pups. Besides getting fresh air, we all hope they'll get tired and sleep when we get back on the road. Whenever there are people at our stops, they always come over and check out the puppies. That's good because the pups will get used to being around strangers.

7

Time Flies

Back home in Texas, the pups are having a great time exploring. We do have to watch out for them at this young age. And we have to teach these little ones about water. My Pals have this big swimming pool that they sometimes splash around in. We can't let the pups get anywhere near it. If they fell in when no one was around, they'd drown like I almost did at the lake. So we always make sure they get safely into the fenced area of the yard. They're okay there. It's been puppy-proofed.

One day Grace calls and asks my Pals if she can come over and see the pups. I'm a little worried. Mel, my pups' dad, is Grace's dog. I've heard that it's standard practice to give the father's owner what they call "the pick of the litter." I'm hoping that Grace won't want one of my babies. Or at least that she won't take one right now. I'm having so much fun with them.

Grace comes to the house and looks my babies over. But she doesn't want one of them. So Don offers her a good amount of money. He says he wants to be generous because of all the help that Grace has given them. Grace looks very pleased and I'm happy too because I can keep my babies, at least for now.

All my careful feeding is paying off! The pups are getting big and fat. They love playing outside and have a great time chasing each other around and wrestling. Then, exhausted, all three of them end up in a little heap. These days with my pups and my Pals are the best of my life so far.

"Licky Lucy" and her brother Killian at about six months.

But changes are on the way. I hear my Pal Don saying it's almost time to part with at least two of my babies. This makes me real sad because I can't stand thinking I'll never see them again. But surprise! It turns out that Patricia's daughter Misti is going to take Killian. She really was my first human mom and I love her. Since Misti lives in Houston, we see her a lot. So now I know I'll see Killian too. What a relief. And there's more good news. Don's son Dan and his wife and kids will take Mak. They live in Wisconsin, so I bet we can see Mak when we're up there. The best news is that Lucy isn't going anywhere. She's staying with us. Forever, I hope. I can tell you, I will sleep really good tonight.

AS IT TURNS OUT, I WON'T HAVE TO PART with any of my pups for a while. Patricia has decided that she wants to show Lucy as soon as she's six months old. And Don says she should make arrangements with Misti to show Killian too.

"We want Sally's Kennel to have champions," Don says.

Wait a minute! What's this "Sally's Kennel" stuff? A kennel is what I go in when I travel. Or it's where Mel and I got together. Or where the vet put me when I was sick. Or where I wait before I go into the show ring. I make it a point to keep listening to my Pals talk and I think I've finally figured it out.

There's another kind of kennel called a "breeding kennel." This is what my Pals are talking about. It just means they are "official" breeders of purebred dogs. They have to follow lots of rules and keep records of everything they do. Otherwise, they'll get in trouble with this "official." I sure don't want that to happen.

Now here's the best part of this "Kennel" thing. My Pals have named their kennel after me! It's called Mustang Sally's Kennel. And there's more! All my pups have Mustang Sally as the first part of their official, registered name. Patricia says everyone loves me and will recognize the name in my babies. So now each of my pups has three names: an everyday name, a Mustang Sally Kennel name, and a pedigree name. How cool is that!

When the pups are about six months old, we head back to Perry, Georgia, for another regional show. Killian and Lucy are signed up for the "Six Month Baby Sweepstakes." Twenty other Staffie pups are also entered in the sweepstakes. But they don't have a chance. My two puppies steal the show. Lucy wins "Best of Breed" and Killian wins "Best of Opposite Sex." You can imagine how proud I am. Some of the other Staffie owners and breeders come over to congratulate Don and Patricia. And me too. It's too bad Mak can't be here. Don's son Dan picked up my boy before we left for the show and took him home to Wisconsin. Now he can start bonding with his new family. I miss Mak, but I know from the pictures that Dan and his wife Patti have sent us that he's getting lots of love up north.

Patricia is determined to make Lucy and Killian champions. We start going to more shows to build up points. My Pals have decided to show only one pup at a time and Lucy goes first. Remember, I was already two years old when my Pals started to show me. But Lucy is only six months old when Patricia starts showing her. Age does make a difference, you know. The judges say it's pretty hard to tell how these real young ones will turn out, so they take their time making them winners. But Lucy becomes a champion before she's even eighteen months old. That's pretty darn good.

Then it's Killian's turn. It takes my boy a little longer than Lucy to make champion. It must be because he has a couple of lower teeth that aren't quite perfect. Pretty picky, don't you think? But I guess the judges have to choose the dogs that come closest to the breed ideal. Once Killian becomes a champion, my Pals decide to retire him. Misti is happy. Now she can have her "baby" around all the time.

My boy Mak looks pretty happy cuddling with his new Pal Tia.

Photo courtesy of Dan and Patti Rashke

WE HAVE A NEW KIND OF LIFE NOW. It's just Lucy and me and we're home most of the time. I love having my daughter with me and my Pals love her too. In fact, sometimes I think Don pays too much attention to Lucy and not enough to me. When this happens, I just have to set him straight. If he calls me to come over, I just stare at him like I don't understand. Then he tries to coax me. After a little bit of that, I do walk over to him, but very slowly. When he starts to talk to me, I turn my head away and pout for a little while. That makes him feel bad and he pays even more attention to me. He starts tickling and scratching me until I finally turn my head for a kiss. When I'm *really* upset with him, I just sit on the couch and refuse to look at him. We have this kind of "standoff" for a while. But it never lasts long. I just can't hurt my Pal Don.

It's starting to get cold—for Texas, that is. I think Patricia will be bringing out the Christmas stuff soon. I'll have to be careful to stay out of the way or she'll get mad. And I'll have to keep a close eye on Lucy, who doesn't know any better.

But guess what? We're going to Wisconsin for Christmas this year. I'm excited because I'm thinking maybe I'll get to see Mak. The trip up in the motor home goes pretty smoothly. Lucy settles right in and, of course, I'm used to it by now. But when we finally get "up north," I realize that "Christmas in Wisconsin" is going to be real different from a holiday in Texas. Because…it is COLD!

I never thought I could feel so cold. Now, I'm starting to envy all the dogs that have long hair to keep them warm. The only way I can keep warm is just grit my teeth and really romp around in the snow. One day, when Lucy and I are outside playing, we decide to run into the woods to explore. What a mistake this is! Besides being cold, everything is white. And everything looks the same. And it's very quiet. After a while, I can't tell where I am, or where Lucy and I came from. I have no idea that my Pals are calling for us. The sounds don't carry through the heavy snow. Now I'm getting really scared.

The snow is almost two feet deep in places, over Lucy's head. We have to keep jumping up in order move around, and I can tell my little girl is getting tired. Don't forget, she's not even two years old. All of a sudden, a big black bear comes roaring out from behind some trees and heads toward us. This guy is a giant—about a hundred times bigger than us—and he's showing his teeth. Poor Lucy is so scared she just curls up in a little ball. I guess she's hoping the bear will think she's giving up and leave her alone. I know better.

Suddenly—like magic—I flash back hundreds of years. This is what my ancestors faced! Maybe the bear is trying to get even for what they did. I'm very scared, but I know I have no choice. I bare my teeth and growl with my meanest voice. Then I run very, very fast right at the bear. I charge past him and circle around. I make a move like I'm going to attack, then I swing away from his huge paw.

I know I'm much faster than this big old bear. By the time he turns to get me, I'm already attacking from the other side. Then, when he turns again, I make another jump and hit him as I push off. He turns toward me and I make another attack. He tries to paw me again but I'm already gone. We spar a few more times. Then, would you believe it, this bear goes down on all fours and just walks away. Of course I'm not going to chase him. I hurry over to Lucy so we can head the other way.

We're both really tired now. We've gotten so turned around that we have no idea where we are. I'm thirsty so I eat some snow. Then I huddle with Lucy, trying to think what to do. All of a sudden, I hear sounds like cars or trucks. We head in that direction and come to it—the road that will take us home. Lucy and I are so happy we start running down the road—towards home.

We're really moving now. Then I hear something wonderful. It's my Pal Don hollering at the top of his voice—from his car, behind us. Lucy and I skid to a stop and turn around just as Don is getting out of the car. He's calling us and we run towards him as fast as we can. He opens the car door and Lucy and I jump in. The heater is on! We are so happy to be safe again with our Pal. Don gets in and then, would you believe it, he turns the car around. Yes, Lucy and I were running down the right road but we were going the wrong way.

I try not to think about what would have happened if we had gone on down that road. My Pals say we're really lucky. We might have been killed. Or starved to death. Or frozen. Believe me, I've learned my lesson. From now on, I'm sticking close to home. No more exploring in the woods.

Before we leave Wisconsin to go back home, my Pals buy a snowmobile. I hear them saying you can even go backwards in it. Why would you want to do that? The man who delivers it shows Don how it works and then he backs it into the garage. Now I understand the "backwards" part. Don says he's sure his son Richie, who takes care of the property when my Pals aren't there, will "break it in." I don't see why they want to break a perfectly good, new snowmobile. Sometimes I just don't understand these humans.

WHEN THE MOTOR HOME IS ALL LOADED UP, Lucy and I jump right in. On the second day of our trip, it starts getting warmer. That makes it nicer when we have to stop for meals and potty breaks. Patricia says it always seems to get warmer around Oklahoma. She's hoping the weather will be just as good when we get home. Me too.

On this trip, Don is taking a new road. He has to stop and pay money at all these different "toll stations" along the way. At one of the stations, there aren't any people around to collect the money. Don doesn't have the exact amount, so he asks Patricia to see if she can find anyone to make the right change.

Just as Patricia starts to open the door of the motor home, the wind picks up and the door flies completely open. Wouldn't you know it, Lucy jumps out and starts running around. Patricia is calling "Lucy, Lucy." Then she yells: "This is a super highway and the cars don't stop." When Lucy goes out onto the road, the panic really starts. Don pulls the motor home forward a little bit, turns the motor off, grabs a leash, and gets out. Just then, a lady in a car stops to help Patricia. The lady starts calling "here puppy, here puppy," and Lucy runs toward her. It's awful watching all this from the window of the motor home because I can't do a thing to help.

Patricia is really beside herself now. She screams at Lucy, who turns and heads toward a hill by the side of the highway. I know my baby is confused by all the yelling. Of course, Patricia is still afraid Lucy will run into the road again. Cars are whizzing by and the lady is still calling "here puppy." Patricia is so upset that she's crying and then she slips and falls down. Meanwhile, Don heads over to the field with the hill. He still has the leash in his hand. Lucy sees him now, makes a mad dash toward him, and collapses right at Don's feet. I think my poor Lucy was even more scared than the rest of us. She just didn't know what to do. At last, I see Don and Lucy coming toward us. I can't wait to start licking her—and Don and Patricia too for saving my baby's life.

AFTER ALL THIS EXCITEMENT, we're happy to be safe at home again in Texas. The weather isn't that warm here, but it's a lot better than Wisconsin. In fact, it's perfect weather for Lucy and me to do one of our favorite things. We take turns going for a run alongside Don in his golf cart. Whenever we hear Don starting up that golf cart motor, Lucy and I go crazy. We give a little cry that says: Please don't leave us behind! We just love to run.

This time, it's Lucy's turn. Don's driving down a street near our house. I'm sitting in the golf cart next to him and Lucy is running alongside on her leash. We're almost past this one house when we see these two great big black dogs. I mean these guys are BIG and they are snarling. And then they come after Lucy. My Pal Don is certainly not going to let them attack Lucy from behind. He stops the golf cart and gives Lucy enough room to turn and face these dogs. My little girl is fearless. She hunkers down her rear end, plants her front legs, and opens up her chest as wide as she can. Then she bares her teeth and a frightening snarl comes out of her mouth. Those two dogs stop in their tracks, turn around, and head back home.

Don gets out of the cart and goes over to the lady standing in front of the house. He's very polite, but he warns her that she better keep her dogs on a leash if she can't control them. That's the law here in Texas, he says. You must have your dog on a leash if it's out in public. Then my Pal turns around, walks back to the golf cart, and we continue our run. I'm not much of a fighter (except maybe with that old bear in the woods). But it turns out that Lucy sure is. We think maybe it's because she's more insecure than me. Maybe it's because she's smaller. Whatever the reason, it seems like since that big scare in the Wisconsin woods, she's ready to protect herself. She sure makes me proud.

8

The Big One

Pretty soon I can feel it getting a little warmer. My Pals say it's almost February. Then they start talking about something called the "Westminster Show" in New York, wherever that is. They're saying how important and "prestigious" this Westminster Show is. They say you can even watch it live on your computer. I wouldn't know how to do that. My Pals say I've done so well in the show ring that it would be great to top it off with a win at Westminster. It sounds like they're planning to go there with me.

Now, I really like to please my Pals because I love them and they're so good to me. But I'm scared because they're talking about flying to this New York place. I don't fly. I know birds fly and sometimes I think the squirrels I chase can fly. But I've never been able to figure out how to do it. Then I hear Don talking about how they need a special type of kennel for me to fly in. Uh oh!

One day my Pals bring this new kennel into the house and set it down in the living room. They want me go inside and get used to it. I don't want to go in that thing. I really hate it. It's not at all like my regular kennel. The sides are solid and you can't look out. That also makes it very dark inside. But my Pals insist. They say I've got to get used to it because we are going to New York and that is the only way the airline will take me. Now I'm really getting scared.

"We've been training for this a long time, Sally," Don says in his quiet, serious voice. "And now the time has come to go and see how we can do at the Westminster Show."

I can tell my Pal is trying to make me feel better about all this. He's petting me and scratching behind my ears. It looks like I don't have a choice.

Don and Patricia line up a new handler to show me. And, of course, we have to make arrangements for Lucy, who's staying at home. I don't want to go without Lucy even though my Pals keep telling me she'll be fine. They say that one of our nice "critter sitters," Tolef, will be here with Lucy at night. And he'll stop in several times a day to check on her and take her out for you know what. I guess she'll be all right, but I still don't like this airline taking me without my Pals.

Once everything's organized at home, it turns out that my Pals and I will be flying to New York together. Except—we're *not* together. I'm in that nasty new kennel and they put it on this ramp that's moving. Then I can hear a door close. It's so dark, I can't see a thing. And there are these strange noises I've never heard before. Then, all of a sudden, we are tumbling around and bouncing up and down and I have to pee. I just lie there in my kennel shaking. I know I'll never see my Pals again. How could they do this to me? After a while it gets quiet and there's no more bouncing. I try to sleep, but I can't. Then all the bouncing and tumbling starts again. Now my ears are hurting and my stomach feels funny. I feel like I'm falling. Then—BANG, BANG—and everything comes to a stop. The door opens and somehow I'm still alive. A bunch of men are talking and they grab my kennel and shove it up onto something. The thing starts moving and soon I'm inside a building. Guess what? Here are my Pals waiting for me! They are happy—but not as happy as I am.

We ride in a car to a hotel that's pretty nice. But it's cold here in New York. Almost as cold as Wisconsin. I don't like doing my business in this weather but "what are ya gonna do?" (I picked *that* up in Wisconsin.) My Pals bundle up and take me to this big puppy park called Central Park.

There are a lot of dogs in this park and it has rolling hills and trees and walkways that people are supposed to use. I can hardly stand this cold air. And they expect me to do my business? No way! Patricia walks me some more. There is no end to this park. Finally, Don says, "Let her off the leash. That should help. She can run to keep warm." Sure enough, it does help and I do my business. But then we have to walk all the way back to the hotel.

I'm finally getting warm again in our hotel room when my Pals say we're ready to go to the show. Don goes down first to get the car he rented warmed up. Then Patricia and I take the elevator down to the lobby. I'm so happy to see that Don is parked right outside the hotel so I don't have to be out in the cold very long.

My Pal drives us to a building that has cars and people all around it. As we're going in, Don says: "This is Madison Square Garden." I don't see any garden, but I've never seen so many people in one place in all my life. It's like all the dog shows I've ever been to put together into one. It's so crowded, you can hardly move. Everyone is polite, but I'm not happy about all this pushing and shoving and standing in one place for so long. Finally, we get to where my kennel is set up. A lot of people start coming by to see me—I mean us. Don or Patricia or my new handler, Lisa, always has to be here to answer questions. I'm already tired of all this and my "class" isn't until tomorrow.

We spend the next two days going back and forth between the big show and the hotel. It's really a drag. Because my show time is later on the second day, I have to spend hours just sitting around and listening to people talk. Most of them don't seem to know much about us Staffies. But they're curious and they ask a lot of questions. Then they want to pet me. Now don't get me wrong, I like to be petted. But enough is enough. Can't they see I'm tired?

It's pretty complicated at these big shows where there are so many dogs. That's why they have to divide us into a lot of different levels to compete. These levels are called "classes." They start with the six-month-old puppies, then the nine-month-olds, then the one-year-olds, then the class bitches, then the class dogs, then the special bitches, then the special dogs. Whew! Remember when I became a champion? That puts me in the special bitches category here at Westminster.

At last, it's time for my "class" to show. My handler Lisa brings me into the ring with the bitches. There are seven of us bitches and seven dogs. The judge has us circle around the ring, the dogs first, then the bitches. On the second round, the judge motions for the dogs to go to the left and the bitches to the right. Woops! What's going on? Lisa leads me to the left with the dogs. Uh oh! There we are standing behind the dogs and Lisa's grooming me with some spray.

This must be a big mistake because the judge doesn't even look at us again. After my class is over, Lisa and I go up into the seats and she says something to Don. He's still surprised and shocked. It all happened so fast. Then, Don takes me back to my kennel. My Pals and Lisa are standing around talking to people who stop by. A young couple tells Lisa that they're interested in puppies. Then they ask her about me. Lisa says: "This girl couldn't win—she's too small."

I can see that Don is listening to what Lisa is saying. And later, I hear my Pals talking about it. They're also wondering why Lisa went the wrong way with me in the show ring. Don says he's going to review my performance on his computer when he gets home. We spend the night in the hotel and the next day we all go back to my kennel area at the Garden, as they call it. My Pals ask one of the other handlers to keep an eye on me while they go watch some of the show. Before they leave, my Pals are flipping through the show catalog and I hear Don say: "Holy Cow! Lisa is also showing a Golden Retriever. She took a Best in Breed with him."

I guess this must be a "no-no" because when Don and Patricia come back to get me, I hear him say: "How can she do that? We paid her expenses, airfare, hotel, food, and her fee for showing and there she is showing someone else's dog." My Pal says he's sure Lisa had all this lined up before we even left for New York and never told us. "And it's all on our nickel," Don says. Whatever that means.

The next day, we leave New York with no ribbons and a bad taste in our mouths. So much for this big Westminster Show and that handler. I'm sure my Pals will never use her again. In fact, Don thinks we should report her. But Patricia says that would just make us look like sore losers. Me, I'm just glad to be heading home. If only I didn't have to fly there.

9

More Little Ones

I'm so happy to be home again with Lucy. Misti often comes to visit and brings Killian, so I get to be with two of my babies. Too bad Mak is so far away in Wisconsin. I hope I can see him this summer.

When Don reviews the video of my show class at Westminster, he's watching closely for my number six, and he sees what happened. He's pretty mad. He calls up Lisa and says he won't be using her any more. Lisa says that the other breeder, the one who owns the Golden Retriever, is willing to split some costs with Don. My Pal says okay, but you're through.

Patricia has found a new handler named Michelle, who lives in Louisiana. She'll be taking Killian on the "show road" again because Patricia never "finished" him. That's another one of those show terms. It just means that Killian hasn't become a champion yet. After a few weeks on the road with Michelle, my son is declared a champion. So now we are a big happy family of champions.

ONE DAY, MY PALS SAY WE'RE DRIVING to Louisiana again. I think we're going to another show, but instead, we stop off to see Killian's handler, Michelle. Then Michelle introduces me to her dog Beau. But hey! I think I already know this boy. Didn't I beat him a couple of times? Then I remember. It was that show in Houston, out in the cold barn. I beat him twice.

Beau looks different now. Older and really handsome. I remember that his show name is Belnore Dream Keeper and he earned the

Number One dog designation. Just like my "husband" Mel did. It looks like I'm keeping pretty good company.

Michelle says, "Let's just get the two of them together and see if they can get along."

That night I join Beau in his kennel. Nothing much happens. We just spend time getting to know each other again. The next day Michelle tells my Pals that it may take another day or so. Don and Patricia decide to go back to Texas. It's only about a three-hour drive and they say it will be no trouble to come back when Michelle calls them.

So that night, Beau becomes my second "husband." He is just as nice and polite as Mel, and I sure hope I'll get to see both of my guys again at some shows.

The next day, Don and Patricia pick me up and we head back home. We haven't been back for long when Don gets sick and has to go to the hospital. I just sit by his empty chair at home, hoping he'll come back to me soon. Patricia can tell how much I miss him. She tries to make me feel better by talking to me and giving me treats, but it doesn't help.

Finally, Don comes home but he's still very sick. I stay right next to him when he's in his chair and when he goes to bed. I just want him to get better so we can play again. And after a while, he does.

I'm so glad Don's better now because I have some other things to worry about. I'm pregnant again and I want to be very careful this time. I'm not going anywhere near the water and I won't eat anything except what my Pals feed me. Remember how sick I got during my first pregnancy? The doctors thought maybe I ate a poisonous flower growing near the lake or maybe some kind of frog. I'm not taking any chances this time.

My Pals have been talking about my delivery and I hear them say I'll have to have another C-section. I'm not too worried. As they say: been there, done that. And sure enough, when it's time for me to go to the vet and have my puppies delivered, it's not too bad. Once you have the little ones beside you, you forget about the pain. And remember, we Staffies have always been very brave. Of course, these three babies are just as cute as my first three. And just like last time, there are two boys and a girl. We've named them Cowboy, Pistol, and Annie. We *are* Texans, after all. My Pals are saying we can't keep all of them and that has me worried, like last time. I hear Don talking on the phone to his son Dan, who has Mak, but Dan says they can't manage another pup. I guess that's good news—for now. All I can do is enjoy my babies while they're here.

With this litter, I know more about what to do for my pups. Like me, everyone who sees them just falls in love—especially with Cowboy. This little guy has four white paws that everyone thinks are so cute. These kids have grown so fast that now they're running and jumping all over the place. I get a big kick out of watching them wrestle each other and growl, as if that little growl could scare anyone.

My Pals are planning to take the motor home to Wisconsin soon. They've bought these neat "modular" fence pieces. You can hook them together in any shape—circle, square, rectangle. And there's a gate you can attach anywhere you want. All the show people use them so they can let their dogs exercise outside off the leash. Now, when we're up at the cabin, my pups can go outside too and still be safe, I hope. Don assures me that we'll all keep a close eye on them. He says it's a good way to train them. When we see any of them doing something inside the fence that they shouldn't, we can just take them out right away before they develop any bad habits.

Even though I think this portable fencing is a great idea, I'm still worried about my pups being outside in Wisconsin. I've heard Don talking about eagles and hawks up there. He says if they get a chance, they'll swoop down out of the sky and scoop up a puppy. Now *that* is scary. I have never seen an eagle or a hawk, so I'm hoping my Pals will watch out for the "kids." Patricia says eagles are beautiful, but that doesn't give them the right to steal my babies. There just seem to be so many things to look out for: cars, black bears, eagles, hawks, water. I guess if I just stay close to Don, everything should be okay.

THE TRIP UP NORTH IN THE MOTOR HOME goes pretty smoothly. Of course, Lucy and I are very experienced travelers. But for the pups, who are just three months old, it's all a big adventure. They sniff out every corner and look out all the windows. And they chase each other around until they fall down in a tired little heap. After a short rest they're ready to go again. I get tired just watching them.

Once we settle in at the cabin, we sure have a lot of visitors. And they sure love my babies. They hardly pay any attention to me, but that's all right. Just so long as they're nice to my pups. The kids (I mean the human ones) who come to visit are sometimes a little rough with them. It's the women who really love to hold and pet them. I know all about this "maternal instinct." But I won't say I'm sorry my Pals are now feeding the pups. All that nursing was getting hard, what with everyone biting and scratching to get their share. What a mother does for her babies, right?

One day, after taking the pups to the vet for a checkup, we stop for some ice cream. This is always a treat for me and Lucy. I know all about ice cream, of course, but my pups are clueless. At first, they don't know what to do with the stuff. But it doesn't take Cowboy long before he's lapping it up like a pro. Of course, then Pistol and Annie sidle over to see what it's all about. Now they're all into it, chasing the ice cream around the dish as it slips away from their tongues. It's fun to watch. I bet next time there'll be no hesitation.

My Pal Don on his favorite toy at the cabin.

The summer is going by so fast. I can hardly believe it's almost time to go back to Texas. But I know it is because the leaves are starting to fall. Before we pack up, Don tries to introduce the pups to the ATV. That's short for "All Terrain Vehicle." It's like a little tractor and Don says it has four-wheel drive. I don't know about that, but it sure makes a lot of noise. Lucy and I are used to the noise because my Pals sometimes take us for a run down the road and back. Don always ties our leashes together so he can hold onto them and keep us safe as we run. But my puppies are scared of this strange, loud thing. And Cowboy is the most scared. Don puts his leash on to take him for a short, slow run down the road, but Cowboy will have none of it. He backs away from the "thing." Finally, Don says, "Okay, maybe next time."

BACK HOME, COWBOY'S GETTING READY to make his debut. I can hardly believe he's almost six months old now. Patricia has given up her role of showing the pups herself until after they become champions. Michelle has agreed to be Cowboy's handler and show him until he makes champion. Don says that won't take long. Patricia still needs to work out something with Michelle in exchange for breeding me to her dog Beau. What they decide on is great news for me. Michelle will be co-owner (with Don and Patricia) of both Pistol and Annie. She will raise, train and show them until they reach champion status. And she can also breed Pistol or Annie, but only with my Pals' approval. I think this is a pretty sweet deal. Now, whenever we drop Cowboy off at Michelle's for a show, I'll be able to see my other two babies. Aren't my Pals great?

Needless to say, Don is right about Cowboy. He makes champion before he's even eighteen months old. Then he makes grand champion before he's two years old. In fact, he's one of only eight Staffies this year to make grand champion. As they say: This kid has it all! The most recent AKC standings have him at number five in the breed nationally. I just know my boy will be number one very soon.

It's just Lucy and me at home now. We spend our days playing in the yard and chasing squirrels. Sometimes, people walk by and talk to us. They're not afraid of us anymore, even when we charge up to the fence to say hi. Lucy is so fast, she always beats me. There's no way I can keep up with that girl. She's built like her Dad, Celebrity Ice Cube, aka Mel. They both have strong legs and a wide chest.

Don says we'll be breeding Lucy pretty soon. He thinks the breeding will be between Lucy and Cowboy, who is her half-brother.

This is the same kind of line breeding that was done with my ancestors. I remember Don talking about it with that English judge, Mr. Roger, a long time ago. And it's the same thing Don used with the cows on his farm in Wisconsin.

I don't see how Cowboy is going to have time to be a proper husband to Lucy. He's always away on the show circuit with Michelle. Even though we haven't gone to all the shows he's been in, we hear how good he's doing. I'm really proud of that boy.

10

Home Alone

Now it's time for Cowboy to be in the big, national Eukanuba Show in California. Don and Patricia decide they want to go see him. But they're not taking me and Lucy. I heard them say: "It's just too complicated."

Whenever my Pals are going to be away overnight or longer, they call our "critter sitters"—Tolef and Carol—to come stay with us. Even though it's not the same as having our Pals here, Lucy and I like our sitters. Especially Tolef. He's very kind and you can tell he really likes us too. Not just pretend. He especially likes Lucy, and that's good. Not everyone feels that way because she's always licking people. In fact, her nickname around here is Licky Lucy. But Tolef doesn't seem to mind Lucy's licking at all. Carol's really nice too. But I think she must take care of a lot of cats. I can smell them!

You know how I feel about cats. I don't know why anyone would like a cat. Today I hear my Pal Don talking on the phone. He's telling his brother Richard about the rat that came into our house the other day. Richard must have said he'd give Don a cat because I hear my Pal say: "No waaay!" Don's like me. He doesn't like cats either.

Today, someone comes to our backyard to take down the tree that Patricia thinks the rat came from. Too bad they won't let me go outside to watch. It all seems a little much to me. I mean, a whole tree? Just because of one rat? Lucy and I could probably take care of my Pals' rat "problem." Remember, a long time ago, my Staffie ancestors sniffed out and killed all the rats in England and saved the country. I don't see why Lucy and I can't do the same thing in Texas.

When my Pals get back from the Eukanuba show, they say Cowboy did well. My boy got an Award of Merit. That's pretty good because he's just a two-year-old competing against the five-year-old dogs. It's very hard for young dogs like my Cowboy to win at these big national shows, even if they have the potential. So for now, we'll just have to settle for his Eukanuba merit award.

IT'S GETTING COLD (TEXAS COLD) AGAIN. Patricia's dragging out all the Christmas stuff, so I guess we're staying here for the holidays. I'm glad we're not going to Wisconsin where it's really cold. Before Christmas, my Pals take a short trip up north to see all Don's kids and grandkids. They're only gone a few days, and Tolef comes to take care of us. I guess Lucy and I have it pretty easy.

After the holidays are over, things settle down again. Now that Cowboy is two years old, my Pals decide it's time to breed him with Lucy. My Pals and Lucy take off for Louisiana where Cowboy's staying with his handler Michelle along with Annie and Pistol. They're going to drop Lucy off and leave her there for about two weeks. It's a little lonesome here at the house without Lucy and we all miss her. But, I must say, I'm enjoying the peace and quiet for a change. After about two weeks, my Pals and I drive over to Michelle's to pick up Lucy. Michelle says Lucy and Cowboy mated, so all we have to do now is keep our fingers—and paws—crossed. I can't believe that my *daughter* is going to have puppies. I know it will be fun for her. She can lick and lick those pups to her heart's content. Patricia says: "Licky Lucy will lick the hair right off those puppies." I'm hoping her pups are as nice as my two broods.

My Pals are telling me that when Lucy's puppies get here, I will be a "grandmother." That suits me just fine. I'm happy to give Lucy some advice—I do have experience, after all. But I'm glad I won't have to worry about feeding the babies or cleaning up after them. All I'll have to do is play with my grandpups. When they get fussy or I get tired, I'll just give them back to their mom.

While we're waiting for Lucy's babies, my Pals take me in for an operation. They say I'm not going to have any more pups myself, so I might as well get "it" done. That way, I'll be more comfortable—no more female problems. It may sound like a good idea, but let me tell you, this operation is no fun. Afterwards, I'm sore all over. And my arthritis doesn't help. I have trouble getting in and out of the car these days, and sometimes I even need help getting up on my couch. But all in all, I can't complain. My Pals love me and take good care of me—except when they force those pills down my throat. That makes me gag.

Lucy is being real sweet to me too. I can tell she feels sorry for me. She's always trying to lick me. I can do without all that licking, but I must admit, it's nice to have her curled up next to me when I'm sleeping on the leather couch. Don and I always used to sit on this couch together. But now it's too hard for him to get up and down. He has a special chair that's more comfortable, so I go and sit in his lap there. That is, until my arthritis kicks in. My Pal and I both know that it's tough getting old.

My Pal Don takes good care of me.

Sometimes, Don massages my legs and rubs my back. That helps. I think he understands I'm in real pain. One night when I come into the bedroom, I'm having a hard time walking because of a cramp in my left hind leg. I look up at Don and I think I see tears in his eyes. I don't think he's actually crying, but he's pretty close to it. Nowadays, he always asks me if I want to go to bed when he does. Patricia always stays up late. But Don knows I get tired earlier just like him. So we are growing old together. Don seems to be feeling a little better now. Maybe I will too.

WE'VE BEEN HAVING LOTS OF COMPANY LATELY. Especially today, which is Mother's Day. All of Patricia's family comes over—her daughters and their husbands and their kids. Cowboy's back for a visit and Misti brings my older boy Killian with her. We all have a real good time. In fact, it's so good that I'm stiff all over now. At one point, I have to go into the bedroom to get away from all the activity. With Killian, Cowboy and Lucy running around the yard, it's just too much. The little human boy they call Tristan is here too. He's afraid of Killian and he doesn't like getting licked by Lucy. The grownups have taught him to say: "No licky, Lucy!" Sometimes, Lucy even obeys him. I know my girl is only trying to be friendly. I get along just fine with Tristan and the children in our neighborhood. Don't forget. Staffies are sometimes called Nanny dogs. We love children. In Lucy's case, maybe a little too much.

Me with a little friend. We Staffies love babies and kids.

Photo courtesy of Jessica Morris

In my opinion, the best part of Mother's Day is getting treats from the table. And let me tell you, with so many people here, the odds of getting things are very good. Everyone is saying how terrific the steaks are, and soon I can agree. After the meal, they all sit around talking and I get a lot of petting. I especially like it when Misti talks to me. She and I go back a long way. I love her almost as much as I love my Pals. But Killian gets so jealous when I'm with Misti. He comes over and pushes me out of the way. Cowboy will do the same thing. These boys think they're the only ones in the world. They can't stand it if you pay attention to anyone else.

At the end of the day, after everyone's gone, I'm so tired. I fall asleep at Don's feet, but he's very careful not to step on me. When I do wake up, it takes me a while to figure out where I am. That was some sound sleep! And guess what? I'm still so tired that I go right back to sleep and I sleep all night until the sun wakes me up! Then I have to get Don up. I know he'll jump right out of bed when he feels me scratching at the sheets.

WE'VE TAKEN COWBOY BACK TO HIS HANDLER, Michelle. He'll be on the show circuit with her for a long time now. It seems so quiet with him gone. When he's here, he's always on the move. He doesn't know how strong he is. When he runs into you, it's like you've been "tackled" by one of those big football linebacker guys that my Pals watch on TV.

Even though Cowboy's bossy sometimes, I still miss him and so does Lucy. She thinks it's terrible that he won't be here when she has her babies. After all, the father should be around to help too. It's not really Cowboy's fault though. He has a job to do and that is to win ribbons. But I do hope he gets a chance to see his babies before they grow up and have to go away and live with other people.

So now it's only Lucy and me again. I can relax in the backyard. All the flowers are blooming and boy, can I smell them. Of course, you know that we Staffies can smell one hundred times better than people, so being outside in the spring is a treat. It looks like summer's coming early this year. Some days the temperature even reaches ninety degrees. That kind of heat is hard to take. I can only stay outside for a little while before I start to pant.

Then this spring storm comes along. There's lots of thunder and lightning. Don's sitting in his chair reading and he can tell that Lucy and I are scared. He tries to comfort us by talking in a calm, quiet voice. When that doesn't work, he lets us get on the bed with him when he takes his nap. But we must be squirming too much because then he makes us get off the bed. Lucy and I go under his desk. It feels safer there and we know he's nearby to protect us if something bad happens. Everything turns out okay and Don says we are just "worrywarts." But my motto is: Better safe than sorry.

DON AND PATRICIA ARE TAKING LUCY to the vet today. He has a way of testing her to see how many pups she has inside her belly. It will be good to know how many to expect. Then my Pals can get out the whelping bed so she gets used to it before her babies are born.

When Lucy and my Pals come back, Don says: "There are no babies coming from Lucy this time." The vet couldn't see any sign of puppies inside her. He told my Pals that sometimes "it just doesn't take." Don and Patricia are really sad because they were looking forward to more babies. Lucy sticks pretty close to me now. I think she has an idea that something went wrong, but she doesn't know what. Maybe she's even grieving, just like I did when I lost my fourth pup. I hope she'll get back to her old self soon. But it's important right now for her to be sad. Patricia says we can wait a year or so and try again.

NOW I'M BEGINNING TO THINK Lucy and I will need Tolef and Carol again. My Pals are planning a big vacation…and it doesn't include us. I hear Don talking about going to Africa on a safari. I listen real hard because I don't know where this Africa place is and I don't have a clue about this safari thing. But it must be pretty special because my Pals sure are doing a lot of planning. Don says this is going to be a "photo" safari. They are packing all kinds of cameras and special clothes that Patricia bought. She keeps checking this National Geographic book to find out how to dress and what to take. It seems like a lot of work for a vacation.

At last my Pals have everything ready. They sure have a pile of luggage. I know they'll be leaving soon because they're giving Lucy and me lots of attention. I hope they're feeling guilty about leaving us at home while they go off and have fun. When they finally leave, the house seems empty, even though Tolef is here. Lucy and I do all the things we always do—play in the yard, eat, sleep. But it's not the same. The time goes by so slowly. Each day, every time I hear a noise outside, I think, "It's them!" I run to the front door and sit down and wait. Now I wonder if they'll ever come back at all. They've been gone so long. Maybe something bad happened to them. Maybe they got hurt in that Africa place. Maybe they don't want to be with me and Lucy anymore.

Finally, one day I hear noise outside and it really is my Pals coming home. Of course, once Don and Patricia are in the house, Lucy's running around like crazy, licking everybody. I try to be a little cool and standoffish when they first come in with all their stuff. Just to let them know I'm not happy about them being gone for so long. But...I just can't help myself! After a couple of minutes, I go up to my Pals and they give me lots pats and kisses and I forgive them for going away.

My Pals have some friends over and talk about their "safari." They pass around a lot of pictures. Lucy and I sit and listen to them talk about the elephant herds that would come close to the "land cruiser." I think that's a big car they drove around in. Patricia tells us all about the time a leopard and her cub came right up to their car while people were talking and taking pictures. Patricia thinks she must have been showing her cub that no one would hurt it. Everyone is asking questions about where my Pals stayed and what they ate. They seem surprised at how well everything went. I think this "National Geographic" person who planned their trip must be pretty smart.

I can't believe it. Now my Pals are planning another trip. But this time it's just back to Wisconsin and the cabin. Of course, Lucy and I are going. Yea! Before we leave, we visit Michelle to see Cowboy and his sister Annie and brother Pistol. What a treat to see my second batch of babies all grown up and together again. Pistol is not anywhere near as big and strong as Cowboy. But he's a real nice looking boy. Michelle has been showing both Pistol and Annie and now they're both champions. But what did you expect? I'm so proud of them.

11

Fun and Games

Not much has changed up here in the Wisconsin woods. I'm glad about that because I really don't like surprises anymore. Lucy and I have the whole place to ourselves. Once we unpack all our stuff and settle in, Don takes the ATV out on the road and lets Lucy and me run on our own alongside or a little bit in front. It feels good to stretch my legs after all that time in the car. My Pal even lets us go into the woods along the road. But he always calls out "far enough" so we know when to come back to him. Whenever we go for a run, Patricia worries that something will distract us in the woods and we'll get lost. I guess she just can't forget that winter up here with the bear. But it's warm now and sound travels well. We can always hear Don calling us.

Sometimes, just for fun, Lucy and I fool our Pal and come out of the woods way in front of him. I think even he gets a little worried when we do this. In his really serious voice, he'll say: "Stay near me." Then he turns the ATV around and we run back home. Running in this warm air makes me tired and thirsty. As soon as we get back to the cabin, I head straight for my water bowl. It's nice and cool in the house so Lucy and I lie down and take a little nap.

What we don't know is that while we're napping, Patricia goes into town and gets some big balls for us to play with. When we wake up, she throws one onto the veranda and Lucy and I charge after it. As hard as I try, I can't get a bite of this ball. So I try a different strategy. I push it into the corner of the porch. But then Lucy comes

After all that running around, it's nice to take a little rest on a big soft pillow.

over and pushes it away. We both chase this pesky thing again and corner it. By now, we're both pretty upset that we can't get our mouths around this ball. And you know that we Staffies have big jaws. Patricia laughs and says to Don: "They're having a ball with this." I think she's making a joke.

All I know is that I'm getting tired again. Lucy is so fast that I can't keep up with her. I try one more time to grab the ball with my jaws wide open. Then I give up and go inside to rest.

The time I like best up here is early morning. My Pal Don hears Lucy and me moving around and he gets up too. The three of us jump in the car and go out to get some coffee and the morning paper. When we get back, if we've been good, Don gives us a treat. Sometimes it's leftover steak from the night before, sometimes fish. I think they bring it back from a restaurant where they have dinner sometimes. Wherever this stuff comes from, it's always good. Don calls my name first and gives me my piece. Then he calls Lucy. That way, we don't have to fight to see who can snap it up first. Sometimes, Patricia forgets to do it this way. Then, because Lucy is so much faster than me, she always gets there first. That's just not fair.

A little later, after we've had our treat, Patricia gets up and has breakfast. Then she takes us for a walk. Usually we behave, but today Lucy and I take off into the woods after a deer. Lucy comes back out right away, but I follow the deer for a while. As Lucy told me later, Patricia gets worried when I'm gone for so long. She and Lucy hurry back to the cabin to tell Don. He gets out the ATV and crosses over the road into a small woods. He yells back to Patricia to wait on the road. Don's calling out as he's moving. He can't see that I'm just behind him. Patricia sees me from the road and comes over to get me. After she puts me in the car, she chases after Don to let him know she's found me. As you can see, even with just the four of us, there's always some excitement around here.

When we have visitors, it gets even more interesting. This weekend, two of Don's sons—Rich and Dan—come up. Rich brings Carley, his year-old Golden Retriever, and Dan brings my son (and Lucy's brother) Mak. The four of us dogs really mix things up. There's never a dull moment. But if it starts getting a bit wild and I want to be left alone, I let Mak and Lucy know that their mom's still in charge. With these kids around, it's a lot of fun. But it can be exhausting and I have to pace myself. One thing's for sure, I sleep really good at night up here.

Later in the summer, Don's brother Richard comes up again and so does Don's cousin, Frank. Frank loves dogs. Back at his own house he has Springer Spaniels, so we get along great. Of course, Richard is still a cat man, but he doesn't mind us. He'd just rather be fishing or playing his horn. Don says Richard is a great writer of books. I'll have to listen up and see if I can get any tips from him. It sure would be great if I could write a book too.

In the middle of the night, when everyone else is asleep, I suddenly wake up. I can just feel that "something" is going to happen. I can always tell when there's going to be a storm or lightning. I hate lightning. Once it starts, I get so scared. I go into the bedroom and paw at my Pals' bed to wake them up. But they're sound asleep. Then it starts to rain real hard and the wind is blowing like crazy. Still, everyone is sleeping. All of a sudden, there's a big FLASH and then a BANG. My Pals jump out of bed.

Don and Patricia and Lucy and I are standing there in the big room, wondering what's happening outside. Then we hear a loud crack and something hits the roof. Don gets his flashlight and goes out to take a look. He's all wet when he comes back. He says the lightning hit a tree. It crashed over right near the edge of the roof. Then it fell down the hill. Don says it doesn't look like there's any damage to the roof. Lucy is still so scared that she jumps up on my Pals' bed.

About this time Frank and Richard wander in to see what's going on. Everyone's relieved that the cabin isn't damaged. Richard is thinking ahead. He says the storm will be good for fishing. He tells Patricia to get up early because the bass will be biting. Frank says: "We'll make breakfast for you when you get back." Now that everything's organized for tomorrow, we all go back to bed.

In the morning when we get up, Richard and Patricia are already out fishing. Don, Frank, Lucy and I go out to take another look at the roof. There's no serious damage. Don says he's going to redo the window frames in metal so the rain and sun won't rot them out. While we're outside we see Richard and Patricia pulling up to the pier. After they tie up the boat and climb onto the landing, Patricia waves at us with one hand and holds up a long chain of eight or ten big fish with the other. Back at the cabin, she says they are all bass. They caught more, she says, but they were undersize, so they threw them back in the water. "For next year," she says. Patricia asks Don to take a photo of her holding the fish to prove to her son-in-law, John, that they are really catching them. John always fishes for "crappies," but Patricia knows that what he really wants to catch is bass. He's always talking about seeing them in the weeds where he fishes.

I think what my Pal Don really likes about all this fishing is that Richard is happy to clean the fish. He's into the whole fishing thing, and cleaning is just part of it. While Richard's cleaning their catch, Frank and Don fry up some bacon, scramble some eggs, and make toast and coffee. Lots of good smells, that's for sure. Then they all sit down for breakfast. Of course, Lucy and I hang around. We know that sooner or later they will give us some bacon, maybe even eggs. Yummm. This stuff is good! Afterwards, everyone wants to go into town. We all jump into the SUV and head for "civilization," as Patricia says. We pick up the mail, gas up the car, and buy a paper, some fish bait, and groceries. Patricia buys Lucy and me a couple of basketballs. Yea!

Back at the cabin, Lucy and I join Frank, Richard, and Don on the veranda. Patricia comes out after she's washed the bass and put them in milk to soak. I guess that makes them tastier. It's cooling down now and there is a little breeze. Everything is just perfect.

Me and Lucy are safe with our Pal on the boat up in Wisconsin.

Maybe it's something about the quiet evening, but everyone starts talking about what they're doing. Frank has helped produce some of Richard's plays in Milwaukee, so they talk about what Richard's working on now. He tells them about the time he was held up at gun point in Washington, D.C., where he lives with his wife and those cats. He says guns are pretty common in some neighborhoods. That's why he wrote a play called "Bang" about young people and violence and gun control. Just then, we hear a bang coming from the woods. Don says: "It's those damn poachers, shooting deer out of season for their meat." I know this is a bad thing. These poachers could get in a lot of trouble and I hope they do. I sure am glad I'm not out there in the woods. They might shoot me too. Some people just don't care about laws.

My Pals and Frank and Richard talk some more. Frank asks Don: "How long will you keep showing the dogs?" Of course, my antennas perk up whenever they talk about us dogs. Don and Patricia say they'll keep Cowboy on the circuit for another year. By age three, he'll have a better chance to become the number one dog for the year. Then Patricia says she still wants to show Lucy and me. She says I'll make a great veteran and she wants to make Lucy a grand champion like Cowboy. That might be fun for Lucy, but I'm wondering if my old bones can take it.

69

Finally we all go inside and have our "fish fry." Even Lucy and I get some. I don't know why they buy dog food. This fish is so much better! After dinner, Don goes over to the fireplace and starts a small fire with some twigs and branches. Then he puts some bigger logs on and gets a real good fire going. Lucy and I love the fire. It's so warm and cozy that it's hard to stay awake. It seems like the fire makes everyone start talking about "old times." Don and Richard and Frank talk about some of the cool things their cousins and kids have done. This gets me thinking about my own relatives. Some of them have been pretty outstanding, especially my own babies.

We're all startled out of our "remembering" by two dogs at our front door. Don goes over to take a look. He says they're both girls and, thank goodness, they're wearing collars with dog tags. My Pals bring them into the house and I can see they are both big Golden Retrievers. Don calls the vet's number on the tags and talks to someone about these two girls. The vet must have called their owner because in a little while a lady comes to our door. She says she didn't even know "the girls" were out. She is so grateful to us. I guess her "girls" are pretty smart. They knew which house to come to for help. I just worry about what would have happened to them if we had already gone home to Texas.

12

Making Plans

When we get back to Texas in late September, there is some good news waiting. Cowboy took Best of Breed in a national dog show in Florida earlier this month. Patricia says, "That's great, but we want him home for a while." He's now ranked number four in our breed. That's my Cowboy! Now we can add another win to Patricia's "trophy room." She's decorated a whole room in the house with all the ribbons and trophies that we've won. And on the walls she has framed pictures of us dogs at all the shows we been in. There's also a pool table in there so people can play a game when they finish looking at all our wins.

Here are just a few of the ribbons we've won that
are hanging in our Trophy Room.

I love looking at all our wins.

After this big Florida win, my Pals talk about showing Cowboy at the Westminster Dog Show in New York next year. All I can say is if they do decide to take my boy there, I'm staying home. But Cowboy deserves his chance. He's at the top of his form now. It looks like he may even be invited to the Crufts International Dog Show held every March in Birmingham. It's not the Birmingham in Alabama. It's the one in England, where I come from!

After they talk and talk and talk, my Pals decide not to take Cowboy to New York. Thinking about their trip with me, they feel that traveling in the winter is just too hard. Also, Cowboy's handler, Michelle, has already planned to take another dog to the Westminster show. At least *she* let my Pals know about her plans up front.

Now that Westminster is out, all my Pals do is talk about the English show. I hear them say they have enough air miles for both of them and a handler. Then they start talking about where to stay and how to get back and forth from the hotel and the show. My Pals have so many questions that they decide to call up the judges from the UK, the ones who helped them when they were just getting started in this "show thing." Maybe *they* can answer some of the questions. Right now, it looks like my Pals and Cowboy will be gone for three weeks. But I wonder about Lucy and me. Three weeks is a long time to be alone.

While my Pals are trying to figure everything out, Michelle comes by with Cowboy. I'm so happy to see my boy! And to know he's finally back with us for a while. I hear my Pals talking to Michelle about going with them to the Crufts show as Cowboy's handler. Michelle seems excited by the idea. She tells my Pals that she has judged American Staffies in Belgium. She knows her way around Europe and could help them with loading and unloading Cowboy as well as showing him.

It sounds like they have an agreement. But what about Lucy and me? I'm starting to worry. Who's going to take care of us?

After Michelle leaves, my Pals talk about getting an application form for the Crufts show. Don says it can all be done by e-mail. I think that's the same way they talk to the English judge, Mr. Roger. My Pals say they're not going to buy any tickets until Crufts says Cowboy can compete.

This must be a pretty complicated trip. My Pals talk about it *all the time*. Don is trying to line up hotels and Patricia is looking at transportation. They sure use their computers a lot these days. That's the first thing Patricia does when she gets up in the morning. I hear Don say: "Maybe you can make a list of all the ways we can get around while we're there and I'll do the same with hotels."

After a couple of weeks of all this computer stuff, it looks like Cowboy's been accepted for the Crufts show. Now my Pals are saying the trip might include more than just England. Patricia's checking on her computer for international dog shows in other countries around the same time as Crufts. She says to Don: "As long as we're over there, why not take advantage of the other shows? Especially if Cowboy does well at Crufts."

But what about Lucy and me? Have my Pals forgotten about us?

Before I know it, Don and Patricia are talking about France and Spain and Belgium. I don't know anything about these places. Then they talk about making airline reservations. Don says that following the "international show circuit" is a wonderful "opportunity" to go to places they'd never see otherwise.

The next thing they're working on is how to register for all these other international shows. Patricia thinks maybe the AKC will have some information. She has to do some more of this research stuff. All this planning is making my head hurt, so I jump on the sofa and lie down to rest. I'm just dozing off when my Pals start talking…again. I hear Patricia say, "It is important to take Sally." My ears perk up. "We don't want to leave her," Patricia says. "What if something happens when we're not around?"

Uh oh. I'm wide awake now. Take me? I hate airplanes. I want to stay here. What could happen to me while they're gone? What are *they* afraid of? *Me*—I'm afraid of this airplane trip. But I also don't like to be here when they're somewhere else far away. And what about Lucy?

Then Don says, "If we take Sally, we have to take Lucy. She wouldn't know what's happening if we're all gone and she's left here alone."

Take Lucy? How's my little girl going to deal with the airplane noise and a new kennel and so many strangers? I don't even want to think about it. And I'm sure not saying anything about it to Lucy. I'm just going back to sleep.

I GUESS EVERYONE DECIDED to sleep on it. But today Don comes into the living room all excited.

"I think we can do it!" he says.

"What do you mean?" Patricia asks.

I'm swallowing hard and wondering the same thing. Don explains that there are several European shows all in a row with time enough to get to each country. Of course, he already has a plan. He says that after the Crufts show in England, we'll take the high speed train under the Channel to Paris, where we'll stay at some place called the Fraser Suites Le Claridge in Paris. Don says that's the best of the best—and they allow dogs. He says that even though we won't earn points like we do at the AKC shows, any wins would be very "prestigious." I guess that means special. Then he says, "We can show Sally as a veteran."

Oh no. Not another "great" idea! Drive me around this Europe place and make me compete too.

The planning seems to be going well, but Patricia starts wondering how long we'll be gone with all these other shows added to the trip. Don says if we enter all the shows, it will be six weeks, traveling mostly by train from place to place. Then we'll use taxicabs at each place to get back and forth from the hotel to the show. But with all the dog food and water and suitcases we'll have to lug around, Don says, maybe we should just rent a car.

I'm getting tired again.

Patricia says it's a good thing we'll have Michelle with us as a handler and helper. But then she asks Don: "How much is all this going to cost? Especially if we have to pay for the handler and her rooms and meals? And three extra weeks?"

Don doesn't have much to say about that. But in the evening he sits down at the table with a pile of papers and his calculator. He must be working on something important because he doesn't even look up or pet me. Patricia's sitting on the sofa reading a magazine.

After a while, Don says to her, "Well, I figured it out financially. Now that we're adding all these other places, we can't afford a handler. You'd have to do all the showing yourself. What do you think?"

Patricia looks surprised. But then she says: "I'm game if you are."

Nobody asks me or Lucy what we think. That's just not fair. But if they did ask me, I'd give them a piece of my mind.

Once my Pals decide they won't be taking Michelle with us as our handler, they have another idea. In the morning Don calls Michelle and explains the situation. Then he asks if she'd be willing to keep Lucy while we're in Europe. He says he knows Lucy would be much happier staying with her and Annie and Pistol rather than alone in the house with just a sitter, even if it was Tofel.

I'm listening hard to all this. Then I hear Don say, "Great!" I guess that means Lucy will be staying with Michelle. I wish I could too.

Lucky Licky Lucy.

I THINK MY PALS FINALLY HAVE A PLAN. Don and Patricia and Cowboy and I will start off in England. Then we'll take a train to Paris and then to Brussels, Belgium. From there we'll go to Leeuwarden, Netherlands, and then to Helsinki, Finland. I don't know how far all this is, but it sounds awesome to me. Patricia's worried that we might get lost. I'm worried that we might not know where to go when we get there, wherever "there" is. I guess we're both worried about the same thing.

Of course, Don says not to worry. He'll make a list of everything we need to do. Then he'll go on the Internet to find hotels and get directions to all the shows. He sure is determined. He even has a map of Europe and he's marked all the places we're going and the roads to each place. Now my Pals are having a discussion about whether to add Berlin, Germany, to the trip. Patricia says why not just fly out of Amsterdam instead of going all the way to Germany? She really doesn't want to go that far. She just wants to keep it simple.

At last, they agree to cut out Germany and Finland and end the tour in Amsterdam. They also decide to rent a car in England and then another one when we leave Paris. Then we can go wherever we want. And, we'll have everything with us in the car. Don says: "We have to start planning what to take along, and don't forget water and food bowls for the dogs."

Now that we know where we're going and how we're getting there, the trip is down to only four weeks. Then my Pals start wondering how we're going to get all the dog food we'll need onto the airplane in Houston. Don decides to ship a sealed tub carrying the dog food and a case of water with our other luggage. Of course, that means an extra baggage fee. We'll also need two kennels for me and Cowboy that meet the international air travel rules.

My Pals are not the only ones worried about the nine-hour trip from Houston to Birmingham, England. I think it's going to be pretty hard on Cowboy and me. Will it be cold and dark like the flight to New York? And who's going to feed us? And how will we take our potty breaks? Nine hours is way too long to hold it. My Pals call Continental Airlines and they recommend putting an absorbent blanket in each kennel for the flight. Then, when we get to England, we can go outside to do our serious business. Oh, *that* sounds nice.

Of course, Patricia is the one who has to do all the packing. But she's cool right now. She just says, "Leave it to me. I'll get it done."

Whew! I'm getting tired just listening to all the stuff my Pals have to do. I hope they don't get into one of their big arguments over this. I don't like it when that happens. They'll start out talking and then, before you know it, they're yelling. I can't always tell if they're really mad or just excited. Right now, I think Don's just happy we're finally going to do this. Of course, Patricia is the one who worries, and I don't blame her. She needs to know exactly what the plans are before she starts packing. I've been giving this "packing" some thought too.

I hope Patricia remembers to pack our matching faux leopard outfits. They ought to be a big hit in Paris. Patricia says that fashion is very important to the French and that it's too bad we can't wear our outfits at the shows. She should know by now that these dog shows are much too serious for that.

THANK GOODNESS WE HAVE A FEW THINGS to distract us from all this "planning" business. Mainly, the holidays. They're always a big thing at our house. This year, Patricia keeps the plans simple for Thanksgiving—just some of her family come for dinner. But before that, we have to shoot a picture for this year's Christmas card. Patricia wants me, Lucy, and Cowboy to be in the photo with her and Don. For our photo session, the three of us dogs have to wear these red and green ruffles around our necks. Don doesn't have to wear a ruffle, but he does have to dress up in a bright red sweater. Patricia gets out two large, carved and painted statues and puts one on each side of the sofa. She says they look like the guards you see at Buckingham Palace in London—the ones with the tall black hats and the red jackets. Well, I guess this makes sense. We *will* be going to England very soon.

The Christmas card photo shoot, 2009. From left:
Lucy, me, and Cowboy with our Pals.

Photo by Brad Meyer

77

Patricia tells Don and me and Lucy and Cowboy exactly where to sit. Then she gives our camera to the friend who has come over to take the pictures. Then she sits down next to Don on the sofa and says, "Everybody smile."

Click. Click. Click. I sure hope we get at least one picture that Patricia likes so we don't have to do this again. I want to hurry up and get to the good stuff—Christmas treats and presents. Maybe we can stop talking about our big trip for just a little while.

AFTER THE HOLIDAYS, THINGS GET REALLY INTENSE. It seems like Patricia has been packing for weeks and "Crufts" is all my Pals talk about. It's a good thing they know the Pughs. While they're planning this trip, Mr. Roger and his wife Doreen give them so much good advice. What to bring. Where to stay. What to expect. And how the whole Crufts system works. They're helping us just like Grace did when my Pals were first getting started in the dog show biz.

After all this talking and planning, March 2011 finally rolls around. It looks like we are really going on this great adventure across the ocean. Everyone but Lucy, that is. She doesn't know how lucky she is. But I'm kind of surprised at myself. I'm starting to get a little excited about this trip. I'll be going back to my homeland after all these years. I don't remember much about it, except leaving. Now I'll have a chance to really look around.

13

The Not-So-Grand Tour

England at last! Here we are at the Birmingham International Airport. It's not that far from where we Staffies started out a long time ago. The plane ride over was no fun but I'm trying to put it out of my mind. And there sure is enough going on here to distract me.

We pick up the rental car we ordered, load it up with all our stuff, and head for our hotel. We'll be staying at the Crown Plaza. It's not far from the airport and it's very close to the arena at the National Exhibition Center (NEC) where the Crufts show is held. After we check into the hotel and unpack, we head over to the arena.

It's only a short walk and, finally, we're at the famous Crufts Dog Show. Let me tell you, this show is something else. Bigger than the biggest shows we have on our side of the Pond. The arena is huge and right away I see *hundreds* of my distant relatives. I don't even try to count them, but Patricia says there must be at least five hundred Staffordshire Bull Terriers here. My Pal Don says this is probably the biggest dog show in the world. He says more than twenty-five thousand dogs will be shown over this next week. I can't even imagine that many dogs all together in one place. Honestly, I'm very relieved that Patricia has decided not to enter me as a veteran in the show. She thinks it would just be too much for me...and I agree.

Now I only have to worry about the dogs that Cowboy will be up against. Patricia goes off to talk with some of the other Staffie breeders. They tell her how the show is set up. When she comes back, she explains it all to Don. Of course, I listen in.

Here's how the show works for all the different breeds—including us Staffies. First, they take all the females competing in a class and break them down into groups of thirty bitches each. The judge selects three bitches from the first group of thirty and they go to a separate ring. Then the judge does the same thing with all the other groups of thirty bitches. After this first round of judging, they end up with about thirty bitches in the separate ring. Then the judge goes over to that ring and has these "selected" bitches line up according to their handler's number. Of course, everything is being videotaped along the way. Then the judge picks out the Best of Breed Bitch and two Reserve bitches from this group of thirty. All the bitches are released and the judge's three picks will be called back later.

The process works the same way for judging the Staffie "dogs," including Cowboy. There are so many Staffies here at the show that they need some fair way to thin out the group. So they go through this with all the Staffie bitches and all the Staffie dogs until they get the numbers down to twenty-one bitches and twenty-one dogs. It will take the judges about three days to get through the five hundred Staffies who are here.

While this Staffie selection is going on, the six other breeds in the Terrier Group that we Staffies belong to are also being narrowed down the same way. I can't believe how all this gets done in just three days, but it does.

On the fourth day, the Staffie judge looks at the twenty-one dogs and twenty-one bitches picked earlier and chooses a Best of Breed (BOB). That can be either a dog or a bitch. The judge also picks two "winners"—a winner's bitch and a winner's dog. At the same time, of course, all the other terrier breeds are doing the same thing.

On the fifth day, the Best of Breed winners for all the breeds competing in the Terrier Group come together and the judge places them 1-2-3-4. The number one dog (or bitch) gets to compete for the Best of Show. There are seven "Group" categories that compete for Best of Show: Hounds, Pastorals, Terriers (that's our group), Gundogs, Toy, Working, and Utility. Right now, these seven "Groups" are made up of dogs from 177 breeds. But this number will change as the Kennel Club of England and the American Kennel Club add new breeds. All these groups have to go through the same process.

Sounds complicated, right? I was confused at first, but I think I've got it figured out now. My Cowboy has to start competing at the very bottom of this process with all the other Staffie boy dogs. He's in the second group of thirty to show. There's so much waiting around and I can tell Cowboy is getting tired of it. Even though there are breaks between showings, who can rest with so much noise? We're all on edge. It doesn't help that not many people are rooting for my boy. The breeders and handlers know Cowboy is an American. They won't be happy if he wins at *their* show.

Don and I are really nervous when it's finally time for Patricia to work Cowboy around the ring. I know she's under a lot of pressure. I think Patricia and Cowboy look real good, but you can never tell what the judge will do. This time, when the judging is over, my Cowboy doesn't win. But he is selected for an "Award of Merit" ribbon. This means he's a really good example of what a Staffie should look like. But I guess the judge thinks he's not good enough. So, it's the end of the road for my boy at this year's Crufts show. He won't be going on to compete for Staffie Best of Breed or Winner's Dog.

Of course, I'm disappointed that my boy didn't win. But I feel really sorry for Patricia. She was so sure Cowboy could win Best of Breed here. Now he won't have the chance to compete for that honor. We're all still proud of our boy and he gets lots of hugs and kisses. Don tells Patricia she did a great job showing him, especially with all the noise and distractions in the arena. He says we couldn't expect Cowboy to take the top prize at such a big show. Besides, Cowboy is larger than most male Staffies. (Don't forget, he's a born-and-bred Texan and we think big.) Don says he doesn't really fit the English preference for smaller dogs—and black ones. I don't see why black is better, but that's what these English judges like. What can you do?

None of this seems to upset Cowboy. In fact, he's pretty pleased with himself—as usual. He doesn't think he did too badly. I can't really blame him. He's still a youngster and he doesn't think about how our Pals feel. At least, with this attitude, he'll have energy for the other European shows coming up.

Even though Cowboy won't be competing for any more honors here at Crufts, my Pals decide to stay until the end of the show. They want to see how the rest of the Staffie, Terrier Group, and other Group competitions go. Then, on the last day, there's the final competition for Best of Show. It's the big prize, so they keep everyone waiting until the very end.

The day after Cowboy's loss, we watch ten Staffies compete in the Staffordshire Best of Breed and Best of Opposite Sex competition. Sure enough, a black male Staffie is selected for Best of Breed. Best of Opposite Sex goes to a Brindle female. A white with black markings gets Winner's Dog and a red and white bitch takes Winner's Bitch.

Even though we didn't win the Best of Breed, we're interested in seeing how the black Staffie winner will do against the other Best of Breed winners in our Terrier Group. Too bad. It turns out that we Staffies won't go any further in the show this year. A Wire Fox Terrier wins the best of group and will be the one to compete from our Terrier Group for the grand prize of "Best of Show."

I'm so glad my Pals decided to stay for the last day of the show. You can just feel the excitement in the air as the seven group winners enter the ring with their handlers. It's the Big One. There's a Griffon bitch for the Hound group. A German Shepherd dog represents the Pastoral group. A Flat-coated Retriever dog is competing from the Gundog group. Of course, the Wire Fox Terrier is representing our Terrier group. For the Toy group, there's a Bichon Frise dog. A Standard Poodle dog is competing for the Utility group. And a Boxer dog represents the Working group.

Everyone is watching the judge as the seven "best of group" winners are put through their paces. I guess I'm rooting for the Wire Fox Terrier so that at least our group will win. It feels like the whole arena is holding its breath. Finally, the judge points to the winner. It's the black, Flat-coated Retriever from the Gundog group. There's lots of clapping and my Pals are checking their program to find out about this dog who won. My Pal Don says he's from Edinburgh, Scotland. His "official" name is Vbos The Kentuckian, but he goes by Jet. That makes sense because he's all black.

NOW THAT ALL THE EXCITEMENT IS OVER, the four of us head back to our hotel to pack up. Then we pile into our rental car and head for London. Of course, my Pals have already booked a hotel room there for the night. Tomorrow we're going to take the "Eurostar" (whatever that is) to Paris. We already have our tickets. My Pals have thought of everything. By the time we get to London and check into our hotel, everyone's really tired. Once we're in our room, Don and Patricia give me and Cowboy our dinner. Then they go down to the hotel dining room for theirs. (Of course, they bring us back a few goodies like they always do.) We all go to bed pretty early so we can get a good night's sleep. We have to get up early for that Eurostar.

In the morning, we take a taxi from our hotel to the St. Pancras rail terminal in London. That's where we get on the Eurostar. Hey, this train is nice. They let us travel in the same compartment with our Pals. Even though Cowboy and I have to stay in our kennels, it's a lot better than being locked up in an airplane hold. This train is also really fast. Things go whizzing by the window so quick that you can't even tell what they are. Then, all of a sudden, it's dark outside and Don says we're going under the English Channel. He tells me that's the deep water that separates England from Europe. What? We're under water now? What if there's a crack in the tunnel and the water pours in? I don't even want to think about that. I'm just going to pretend it's nighttime and take a little nap.

When I wake up, we're still traveling. Don says this is the fastest way to Paris, but it's sure taking a lot longer than I thought. I needed to do my business a while ago. I hope we're getting close because I can't hold it much longer.

Finally, our train pulls into the Gare du Nord in the middle of Paris. Bonjour! We're here!

Of course, right after we get off the train, Cowboy just stops at the nearest wall and cocks his leg. Typical boy! Don heads over to the auto rental place and Patricia takes me and Cowboy through the train station and outside. What a relief.

The traffic in Paris is scary. Patricia always worries about driving in foreign countries, so Don tries to keep her calm by driving very, very carefully. At last, we get to our hotel. If I remember right, it's called Fraser Suites Le Claridge. I'm trying to repeat what Patricia said, but I'm not sure I have it right. I don't speak French, but Don does. Well, a little. Patricia says our hotel is on a street called the Champs-Elysees. That sounds pretty fancy to me. I wonder if they'll let us dogs walk on this street? Of course, Cowboy isn't paying any attention to these finer things we're talking about. He's just looking for his next meal or treat.

I also wonder how these French people will react to us Staffies. Will they be afraid of us, or will they just be good dog lovers? We're in the hotel lobby now, so I guess we'll find out soon enough. Don goes up to the reservation desk and asks, "S'il vous plait, our rooms?" A nice reservations clerk says, "Oui, monsieur, I speak English. You have very nice looking dogs there. What breed are they?" This sounds like a good start. While Don and the clerk are talking, Cowboy and I are checking out the lobby.

This is a pretty nice hotel. We have what they call a "suite" with two rooms. I wonder if one is for my Pals and one is for Cowboy and me? Now Don and Patricia are trying to figure out where the dog show is held and how to get there. Ah ha, Don says, here it is: Parc d'Exposition, Paris Nord Villepinte at 95970 Roissy Charles-de-Gaulle Cedex. Boy, that's a lot to remember. Don decides to ask at the desk for directions and a map. I can't wait to see this place! I wonder how it compares with Crufts?

After settling in our rooms, we all go for a walk on the streets of Paris. Everything is so different here. Cowboy and I have to stay on our leashes to be safe. The cars are everywhere and they go so fast. I think the people are kind of cold. No one stops to pet me or talk to me.

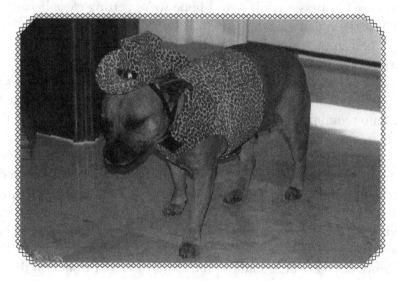

Bonjour! Me all dressed up in Paris.

What I do notice is that most Frenchmen want to talk to Patricia. They ask her all about Cowboy and me. They won't bend down to pet us, they just hang around and talk. This seems kind of funny. In America, most people are interested in us dogs. In France, they are more interested in Patricia. Don says that's the way Frenchmen are. They see a beautiful woman and they can't think of anything else! Don says that's why we had to save them in two wars.

IN THE MORNING, WE CHECK OUT the Expo Center. It's not as big as Crufts, but there are sixteen rings in this place—enough room for a lot of dogs. Cowboy is looking really good now that we've rested up. I sure hope I don't have to compete. I haven't heard Patricia say anything about it, so I think I'm safe. Cowboy shows at 9:00 a.m. tomorrow. I know Patricia will dress up nice for this Paris show. Everyone seems to like her, so maybe Cowboy has a better chance here. But I don't think Don likes French people. He says they are snooty and stuck-up and they treat Americans with contempt. I haven't noticed that, even though they won't pet us. I hate to say this, but I think maybe Don has an attitude. Patricia just says, "Let me do the talking." I think that's a good idea. French people like her, and this way maybe we can get better treatment. Maybe they will even decide to pet me.

Tonight, my Pals go out for dinner. When they get back, Patricia says it was one of the best meals she ever ate. Don's carrying a "doggy bag" so Cowboy and I can have a good French meal too. I agree with Patricia. It's delicious! Cowboy doesn't say anything. As usual, he just gobbles it down.

We wake up early in the morning and Patricia is busy getting ready. While she's doing her hair, Don takes us out to the park. It will be a long day and we need to get our business out of the way. Then we head over to the Center and start getting Cowboy ready to show. I'm listening to Don explain how it will work. There are thirteen Staffies competing—nine dogs and four bitches. The "class" dogs (those who aren't champions) are judged first. There are five of them. The one "class" dog that gets the blue ribbon will come back into the ring to be judged with the "specials" (champions).

Now the five dogs—four specials (including Cowboy), plus the one class dog—and two female specials go into the ring to be judged.

The judge circles around, looking at them from every angle. He stops first at Cowboy, then at a brindle. He has everyone circle the ring. Then, he motions to Patricia to take Cowboy out of the lineup. Yes! Best in Breed! Number One! Then the judge selects one of the bitches for Best of Opposite Sex. Patricia says this means Cowboy will go into the All Terrier Group judging later in the day. I'm so proud of my boy.

Uh oh! Now my Pals say it's my turn. Patricia wants to show me here as a "veteran," just like she was thinking about doing at the Crufts show. She made the right decision there and I was hoping she'd do the same thing here. No such luck. But maybe it's not so bad. It's different here in France. I'll be competing against veterans from other breeds in the Terrier Group, not just Staffies. What I like about these veterans' classes is the great audiences. No matter where we are, the people always clap and say nice things to us "oldsters." When Patricia and I go into the ring, I let myself think: "This is all for me!" Then I'm really walking tall. It doesn't even matter when I don't win.

While I've been working my you-know-what off in the veteran's class, Cowboy has been taking a nap. But I don't mind. It means he'll be good and rested when he goes into the ring for the Terrier Group judging. There are about thirty different types of terriers in this group. The judge is a lady who wears glasses way down on her nose. I don't know how she can see through them when they're so far away from her eyes. But when she bends down to get a close look at a particular dog, she moves them farther up her nose. Then she makes each dog step out one at a time. I can see that she spends more time looking at certain ones. Then she selects seven dogs and lets the others go. Guess what? Cowboy makes it into the final seven! This is awesome. It means he is still in the running for Best of Terrier Group. In the end, however, the judge picks a Norfolk terrier as best of the Terrier Group. I'll never understand how you can compare one kind of terrier to another. We're all so different. But I have to admit, that Norfolk terrier is kind of cute.

Now we go over to watch the Best in Show judging. Just like at Crufts, there is one dog from each of the seven groups. Cowboy and I are just lying low. We're tired and not really paying attention to what's happening in the ring. Then I hear my Pals say, "Oh boy," and my ears perk up. Guess what? Patricia says the judge just picked a Toy Poodle as Best in Show. I'm not surprised, but I'm not happy either. I don't like poodles to begin with. I think they're very snooty. But now I *really* don't like them. I think some countries slant the judging to favor their own native breeds. But, hey, there's nothing you can do about it. At least we won best Staffie. Now we're packing up for Brussels. Maybe we'll have better luck there.

DON GETS MIXED UP IN TRAFFIC trying to find his way out of Paris and onto the highway heading north toward Belgium. Finally, we find the right road and we're on our way, speeding along through the rolling hills of the beautiful French countryside. On the ride, Don and Patricia are talking about how the Belgian dog shows always feature their "national" dog, the Belgian Sheepdog. I'm looking forward to seeing this dog. But all of a sudden, all I can see is FOG. Then Don says to Patricia: "I think we're in some kind of sandstorm."

It seems to be getting worse. Don's trying to use the wipers to clear off the windshield, but they're not helping. I can tell by the sound of her voice that Patricia is getting a little scared. So now I'm scared too. She says to Don, "Maybe we should stop and wait for the storm to clear up." I think that's a good idea, but how will we know where to stop? I can't see anything out of the side windows. Now the sand is hitting the car really hard. Even Cowboy looks worried. We're both squirming around in the back seat trying to find a good place to hide.

Finally we come to a small town. Don sees a sign up ahead for some kind of inn or tavern. He parks as close to the door as he can because the sand is coming down heavier than ever. Then he jumps out of the car and runs into the building. He's in there quite a while and we're all getting worried again. Finally, the tavern door opens and Don yells that we should come in too. But we can't figure out how Patricia can get me and Cowboy out of the car together. Then Don runs up to our car and jumps in. He says we're in the middle of a volcanic ash storm. We need to get inside and see what the news says about traveling.

My Pals put the leashes on Cowboy and me. Then they discuss how we should all get out together and run inside as quick as we can. The plan is to open the car doors at the same time and run to the door of the tavern. The owner is going to hold it open for us. So now Don's holding my leash and Patricia is holding Cowboy's. We all manage to jump out of the car at the same time. Don and I run straight for the tavern door. Patricia's on the far side of the car and she starts to come around with Cowboy. Don and I are just about inside the tavern when Patricia slips on the ash and drops Cowboy's leash. Uh oh!

Patricia tries to grab the leash but Cowboy has jumped away. Don is calling for her to hurry but, of course, she can't. Now Cowboy is running in the opposite direction. I'm inside the tavern now. Don closes the door on me and goes out to help Patricia. I can hear him yelling for her to go inside the tavern. She's yelling back that she can't see Cowboy anywhere. Finally, Patricia comes into the tavern alone. I can still hear Don yelling outside: "Cowboy! Cowboy!"

After a few minutes, Don comes in to rest. The news is on the TV. The announcer says that a volcano in Iceland erupted and sent volcanic ash 60,000 feet into the air. And now that same ash has blown over to northern Europe. Imagine that! Don's says it looks pretty bad. But I'm thinking, how are we ever going to find Cowboy in this storm? I'm so worried about my boy out there all alone.

The tavern owner offers Don some goggles so he can go out again and look for Cowboy. Now my Pal's been out there for an hour and I'm wondering what's happening. I can't see much through the window because it's so dark out. The tavern owner turns on the outside lights, but it doesn't help much. Patricia is worried that Don won't be able to find his way back. Then, the thought of losing Cowboy makes her cry.

Suddenly, the door swings open and a whole bunch of sand comes flying in. Along with all the sand is Don! Cowboy is in his arms, wrapped in Don's coat to keep the sand out of his eyes. Don looks really tired. He sits down and asks for a bottle of water. I guess all that sand made him really thirsty. Patricia is on the floor with Cowboy, wiping the sand out of his eyes and his coat. Of course, I go up to my boy, touch my nose to his and give him a little lick so he knows how happy I am to have him back. Then, I sit on the floor a little ways away so I won't disturb Patricia while she's taking care of Cowboy. I'm sure she knows what to do. At home, she always gives us our medicine and takes good care of us.

Now Don is on the phone with the airline people. He's asking them where we can go to get a flight back to America. Uh oh! We're going to be flying again. I know what that means. Cowboy and I will be inside our kennels in the airplane hold. Don calls over to Patricia and says we may have to go back to Paris because the Amsterdam airport has cancelled all flights. He says we'll have to leave right away.

"How can we go in this storm?" Patricia asks.

Don says we really have no choice. The storm could last for more than a week. If we wait, we may not be able to get a flight from Paris. It looks like this is the end of our European dog show vacation.

One more look outside and even Don is wondering how we can drive back to Paris in this storm. Then the tavern owner pulls out a map and shows my Pals a better route to take on a much bigger highway. He says we'll have better "visibility." Even if there are blind spots, we should be able to see well enough to get out of Belgium and back to France to catch our flight. I sure hope so. I want to go home.

14

Hello Texas!

Yes! We made it back from Europe. I didn't even mind the plane ride because my Pals told me we were finally going home. I hope we never have to go back to Europe. It's just too much for me. I think Don is about to give up on that kind of travel too. He can still get around, but he uses a cane now.

The day after we get home, my Pals go to pick up Lucy at Michelle's. I can tell you, when my little girl walks through the front door, I am so happy. Now Lucy, Cowboy and I can go out in the yard and play almost any time we want. It's always fun having Cowboy in the mix. When he and Lucy aren't chasing squirrels, they take turns chasing each other. I don't really understand what kind of game they're playing. Of course, I can't keep up, but I get all excited just watching. Then I try to catch them. But when I get close, they both run off. Cowboy is behaving pretty well these days. He knows better than to "take me on." He's turning out to be a really nice boy because he's learned to listen to his mother, especially when I growl at him.

THIS EVENING SOME OF MY PALS' NEIGHBORS come over for dinner. But before they eat, everyone goes out back to the gazebo for cocktails. While we dogs are playing in the yard, I hear my Pals and their friends talking about the new regulations for kennels in Texas. It seems like there are going to be new rules that will affect Mustang Sally's Kennel.

Don says Texas will require all breeding kennels to register, pay a fee, and obey certain rules. My Pal says that means kennel buildings and the compartments inside for the dogs will have to meet certain "specifications." He says he thinks they're doing this to get rid of those awful "puppy mills." And it will make all owners and breeders more responsible. I sure won't argue with any of that. But for us, the new rules mean we won't be advertising as "Mustang Sally's Kennel" anymore. Then Don looks down at me and says: "But they'll still be Mustang Sally's boys and girls." I can live with that!

I know our neighbors here tonight love us dogs. We never cause them any problems. We only bark when we see other dogs going by. And it's only to say, "Hello, come and play." And if our neighbors are walking by, they always come over and pet us through the fence. And we never stay outside and bark for no reason. Our Pals would never let us do that.

Maybe it's the people with those tiny little dogs who are stirring things up. We've seen them causing trouble more than once at the shows. They don't like us and they call us "bully dogs." Maybe they're confusing us with Pit Bulls. Well, we do share some of the same ancestors, I'll admit. And we look a little bit alike. But we are very gentle. We Staffies wouldn't hurt a baby and we wouldn't hurt one of these little dogs either. But I also think Pit Bulls have gotten a bad rep. We should be blaming the people who breed them and treat them bad and force them to fight to the death just for entertainment and making money. I've heard this happens a lot in Texas. It makes me so mad. When Don is talking to our neighbors, he says that the AKC is against blaming a specific breed for bad behavior. I agree. It's not the breed. It's the owners, stupid!

TODAY, SOME BREEDERS COME OVER to our house to talk to my Pals. They're interested in having Cowboy as a stud for their kennel females. Of course, they want to know about *my* bloodline. Don brings out my pedigree and explains how my ancestors go way back to breeding in South Africa. He tells them my family name, Maktoum, comes from an Arab sheik. He also explains how the line breeding among my ancestors has preserved many of the best features of my extended family. He tells them how he and Patricia have continued this line breeding so these same great features will be passed on to my babies and grandbabies. I think these breeders are pretty impressed.

Now Patricia takes over the meeting. She's all business. She says she needs to see their bitches' health records and pedigrees. Then there's a lot of discussion about "conformation." That means the physical characteristics of our breed, including teeth, head shape, and topline. The topline is the line of the back. Even I know that a nice straight topline in a Staffie means that the back is straight and strong and healthy. It's a trait that breeders want to pass down from one generation to the next.

Patricia tells our visitors that if their females have been bred before, they'll need to be tested and certified free of venereal disease. Because Cowboy has been bred, he'd also be tested and certified. She also tells them that Cowboy is clear of all the normal problems like cataracts and L2HGA. These breeders know all about cataracts and L2HGA. But I've also learned about some of these health problems that we dogs might have. I always listen when humans are explaining things. Especially when I'm at the vet or at a dog show where people are talking to newcomers. I know that cataracts can make people and dogs blind. And L2HGA can cause changes in a dog's behavior just like dementia in people.

Then Patricia and the breeders get down to negotiating the fees and expenses. Patricia says there will be transportation and boarding expenses. They depend on where the breeding takes place. If it's going to be done at the females' kennel, the breeders will have to show that it has heat and air conditioning. At this point, the breeders take out some photos of their kennel.

Because there are already three of us dogs here at our house, Patricia explains that our community rules won't allow any more dogs. Everyone agrees that the best plan is for Cowboy to go to the breeders' kennel. Then, Patricia starts calculating again. The breeders live in Georgia, so there is the cost of traveling there. And Patricia says they will need to use Cowboy's regular dog food. Don and Patricia would take Cowboy to Georgia by car. Lucy and I would need to have our "sitters" for three nights: one overnight on the way to Georgia; one night there at the kennel; and one night on the way back. I think Lucy and I can handle that. After all, Cowboy has to do his thing and continue the Maktoum bloodline.

Patricia says the travel would be three hundred dollars and the stud fees would be two thousand. She asks the breeders if that's the price range they were thinking of. Of course, I know Patricia isn't about to lower her price, but she wants to let them give their input. They agree on the price. So now it's time to set up a schedule. Patricia says: "Let us know when your bitch starts her cycle. Then we can determine when to bring Cowboy for the breeding." Of course, everything depends on the bitches' cycles because the breeding must be done on the thirteenth day of the cycle. Patricia asks for a down payment to ensure that Cowboy won't be busy somewhere else during that time.

After the breeders leave, Don tells Patricia how well she handled everything. I have to say that all these discussions have tired me out. I say: Just do it! I don't remember dealing with all this stuff when I was bred.

THE NEXT DAY WE GET A CALL FROM DON'S SON DAN. Remember? He and his family are the Pals of Lucy's and Killian's brother Mak. Dan wants to know if we can all come up to his vacation home in the mountains of Colorado, wherever that is. It sounds like a great idea to me. Lucy, Cowboy and I will get to play with Mak and see this Colorado place. Don says it's one of the best vacation areas in the U.S. Dan and his family go there to ski in the winter and just to relax and explore in the summer. Dan says they have an SUV there so all we need to do is fly into the local airport. I don't know about flying again. I think I've had enough of that. Even Don isn't sure. He says it would mean changing planes. He's leaning toward driving. He says the route is very "scenic." Huh?

Now that our transportation is settled, I can start planning. I know Lucy and I can fit easily in the back of our SUV, but this time we also have Cowboy. He's such a "bull." He always wants his own way. I guess we'll just have to put up with him. I think this trip is worth it!

I really don't know how my Pal Don figures out how to get to all these different places. He's going to Houston today to pick up something called a Trip Tik. It will help him map out the way to Colorado. Patricia says, "Why don't you just use MapQuest on the computer? Then you won't have to drive all the way into town." They argue about this for a while and I just sit here looking back and forth from one to the other. They talk and talk and talk until, finally, I fall asleep.

When I wake up, Don's back with all these maps spread out in front of him. He's figured out the best route, so I guess we're about ready to go. All we have to do is pack. At least this time, when my Pals bring the suitcases out, I can relax. I know me, Lucy, and Cowboy will all be going along too. We won't be left here by ourselves while they go off and have fun. Lucy hasn't quite figured this out yet, so she's all nervous and fidgety. Cowboy's cool. He can't be bothered with worrying.

But hey, wait a minute! I see we are packing heavy clothes for this trip. Does this mean it will be cold in Colorado? I'd like to ask my Pals about this but, of course, I can't. I'll just wait and listen and maybe they'll say something about the weather in Colorado. I guess if Mak can stand it, so can we. I just hope it's not so cold that we freeze our paws like I did one time in Wisconsin. That hurt so much.

15

Climb Every Mountain

My Pals are right. The trip through these Colorado mountains is great. And I don't have to worry about airplanes. When we pull up to Dan and Patti's house, Mak is out there to greet us. My son comes right up to the car door. He has no idea that I'm a little worried by all the snow on the ground. When everyone finally gets out of the car, it's quite a reunion. There's lots of hugs and licks and tail wagging all around. Mak and the human kids, Quinn and Tia, start to play with me and Lucy right away. All five of us are jumping around in the snow having a good time. At first, Cowboy's not sure about this cold, white stuff. But when he sees how much fun we're having, he can't help but join in.

Dan and Patti's condo sits on the side of a mountain. It's a beautiful place and it looks like there's lots of room inside. Dan already has a fire burning when we come in from the cold. We're all pretty tired after so much jumping around in the snow. Mak heads straight for the fireplace and stretches out in front of it. And it doesn't take me, Lucy, and Cowboy long to plop ourselves down right next to him where it's cozy and warm.

While we dogs are snoozing by the fire, everyone else is talking about going skiing tomorrow. Well, except for Don and Patricia. They plan to watch the skiers come down the mountain from Dan's back "deck." (That's what they call a veranda out west.) I'm a Texas girl so I sure don't know how to ski. I'm going to stick with my Pals on the deck and just watch. I think Lucy and Cowboy will be staying

Mak's got the right idea.
Photo courtesy of Dan and Patti Rashke

there too. I'm not sure whether Mak can ski. He's not letting on, so we'll have to wait until tomorrow to see what happens. Right now, I'm just looking forward to having my dinner and getting a good night's sleep.

The next day, it's Dan, Patti, Quinn and Tia who head out to the ski area with all their equipment. Dan has his cell phone and he's going to call us when the four of them are ready to ski down the hill past the house. When Patricia gets the call, she and Don and all four of us dogs run out to the deck. There they are! They sure are coming down that mountain fast. Quinn is in the lead, Tia next, and then Patti, with Dan bringing up the rear. They wave to us and we wave back. Well, the humans wave and we dogs chirp like crazy and wag our tails. The snow blows up around their skis as they turn this way and that way. It looks like fun, but I know I could never do that. I can't even run that fast. The snow makes me think of that scary time Lucy and I got lost in the Wisconsin woods with the bear. I thought we both were going to die, but my Pal Don saved us.

We stay out on the deck for a while and then we see the whole family—Dan, Patti, Quinn and Tia—up in the air! They're holding onto some kind of bar as they ride back up to the top of the mountain. Maybe that's the ski lift they were talking about. Whatever it's called, they must not be afraid because they're all waving at us. I sure would be scared high up on that little bar.

When Dan, Patti, and the kids come home, Patricia has some hot chocolate ready for them and treats for us dogs. Then we all settle around the fireplace again and listen to stories about the snow drifts and the jumps they had to make on the ski slope. This Colorado place is just right for them—kind of like our Wisconsin cabin. It's someplace different to go and have fun.

ON OUR WAY BACK TO TEXAS, I think about all my kids. And it looks like there will be more. My Pals have been talking to their handler, Michelle. She wants to breed Annie, who's from my second litter, to Killian, who's from my first. This should be a good mating because they both have my genes. Annie's babies will be another example of line breeding. Michelle also says she will start showing Pistol whenever Cowboy retires. Wow! This is the first I've heard about him retiring. It will be nice to have my boy around all the time.

As we get closer to home, Don gives us the latest weather news. They're saying it could be a bad year for tornadoes and hurricanes. Everyone should take "precautions." I don't know what all these "precautions" are. Maybe they are the same as plans. Don says we all may have to go into the laundry room at home, where there are no windows. If we do, I'll make sure my Pals bring plenty of food and water. As long as we can eat and drink, it shouldn't be too bad. At least we'll all be together. But I wonder where we'll do our business?

While we're still on the road, we get another call from Michelle. She says they may have to move out of their house because the rivers are flooding. They might have to take all their dogs and live in their motor home and a van they have. Patricia starts naming the rivers that are over the levees—the Mississippi, the Ohio, the Missouri.

And she says the flood plain in Louisiana will be covered with water when the dam is opened. This sounds like a very scary thing to me. I just hope Pistol and Annie will be all right. Maybe my Pals should go get them and bring them to our house.

All I know is that I don't like water. I can't swim and the last time I fell in, I sank right down. I don't want to do that again. I hope Don and Patricia make sure we are far away from those floods. I guess they'll make the right decision for us. It just seems like everywhere we go there is danger. The woods when the snow is high. The swimming pools. The thunderstorms (they really make me nervous). The rivers, the hurricanes, the tornadoes. We sure have to watch out for a lot of things.

I think when we get home, I'm just going to go to bed and sleep. That way, I'll forget about all these problems. It's a good thing I have Lucy and Cowboy with me. They keep me busy, but I do miss Killian and Mak and Pistol and Annie. I wonder if Don and Patricia have had any children together that they miss too? They never say anything about this. Of course, I know that there are lots of kids that each of them have. They're all over the country, but my Pals manage to see them pretty regular. That's important for people and for dogs.

16

A Big Decision

Now that we're home in Texas, there's good news. The flooding will not affect the higher land. That means Pistol and Annie will stay good and dry. Boy, we really lucked out on that one. I just hope there are no more emergencies.

This is turning out to be the hottest spring we've had in a long, long time. Don keeps talking about record "highs" all over. I don't know about highs, but it is really hot outside. I wish I was brave enough to do what Killian does whenever Misti brings him over for a visit. He goes to the edge of our pool. Then he goes down onto the first step leading into the pool and lays right down there in the water. He always chirps for Lucy and me to join him, but we always say "no." Lucy would probably be okay sitting with Killian on the top step. She did fall into the pool one time, but she is so strong that she pulled herself right out. But ever since, she's been afraid of the water. I think she's a smart girl to learn from that experience—just like her mom did.

We have lots of things to take care of here at home. This week, I go to the vet to get my vaccinations. He also checks to see how bad my arthritis is. The vaccination shots make me sick for a day or two. The arthritis medicine from the doc is also hard on me at first. But after a bit it lets me run again without hurting all over. So I guess it's worth it. I've noticed that I do get tired faster. That's why I take a nap whenever my Pal Don does, which is just about every day. He's still using a cane. I'd like to have one too. It would help my back left leg. Whenever I lie down for a while, that leg gets really stiff. Then, when I get up, I have to hobble along until my muscles start to loosen up. I guess it's the same with my Pal, except the cane helps him move along faster.

Don watches over me all the time. Take going out back to play, for example. Don lets Lucy and Cowboy out the back door and they both charge down the steps into the yard. But Don takes me out through the swimming pool area so I don't have to go down all those steps. And also so I don't get run over by Cowboy. He lets Patricia and me sleep longer in the morning too. When I do get up, I'm just starving. I eat almost everything I can get my paws on. In fact, it seems like I eat more now than I did when I was younger and more active. I don't know why that is, but at least I'm not gaining any weight. Patricia says I still have my nice "cut." I think that means I'm in good shape.

Today, while I'm out in the yard, I start rolling around in some sand. This always feels so good. But all of a sudden, something is biting me. Then, there are more bites, lots more. Boy, do I get out of that sand fast. And I'm running around the yard trying to shake off those darn things that are biting me. Don sees me running in circles, comes over, and grabs me. My Pal says he has to kill those "red ants." I guess they stung me pretty good because Don has to take me back to the vet for some special shots. The doc said I could die if I had a lot of those bites and no medicine. Whew, another close call! You'd think I would know better by now. No more sand for me.

KILLIAN COMES TO STAY WITH US for the weekend while Misti takes a short vacation. I'll tell you, he's a handful at first. He just flies all over the place. He and Cowboy are always competing. Each one wants to be the "dominant male." I'm not sure who wins this time around. These boys can make life a little rough for me and Lucy. They always want to be first, especially when it comes to food. Most of the time, I just try to give them all the room they want. I know my Pals will watch out for me and Lucy. We're their "girls."

It's just too bad Cowboy and Killian don't seem to understand that I'm their mother and they shouldn't be pushing me around. But I can tell you this, if they get too rough around me, I just give them my "mother growl" and they back off. Those two boys also compete to see who can "mark" the most places. Isn't that silly? I've tried to tell them they better not do that in the house or they'll catch a good one from Patricia. Even I shudder when she gets mad at them. Sometimes I think: Oh my, she's going to kill those boys! But, of course, she never does.

Today, Patricia is sending several of our carpets out to be cleaned. She's not sure if they've been marked. But, as she says: "I won't have anyone saying they smell something on my carpets." I don't blame her. Lucy and I would never be that crude. And we sure don't like these boys marking all over the place either. Patricia has to give Cowboy and Killian several good thrashings with the rolled up newspaper. (The sound of it is worse than the hurt.) With the paper and some kennel time, Patricia makes her point. Those two boys finally catch on that marking in the house is a no-no. Life settles down and we all can have some fun.

I think Cowboy is finally getting used to spending more time at home now. And it's usually nice to have him around. But that boy really needs a lot of petting and attention. He just can't help it. He's used to special treatment from all his admirers on the show circuit, and he expects the same at home. This doesn't sit too well with Lucy, who is now number three in the "getting attention" department. Poor little Lucy.

Now it looks like these changes will be permanent. At just three years old, my Cowboy has decided to retire from show business. My Pals think it's a good idea too because there is no way he can earn enough points to become number one. Some of his competitors just put so much more time and money into winning than my Pals are willing to do. Don and Patricia have other interests besides just dog shows—like travel and visiting their kids and grandkids. To me, these seem like really important things too.

Besides, as my Pal Don explains it, some of these breeders/competitors become AKC certified judges. Their dogs may have an advantage over Cowboy when they're in the show ring with judges who are their friends. So Don says, "Why fight it. Let's just drop out without a big announcement. We'll take Cowboy's 'Number Five in the Breed' and 'Grand Champion' designations as a very good run at it."

I totally agree. Just think, among my six "babies" are five champions and one grand champion. And Mak is without doubt one

Patricia with five of my champion "pups." From left:
Pistol, Annie, Lucy, Cowboy, and Killian.

Photo courtesy of Aafke Goor

of the best pets anyone could have. My kids and I are so happy we could do this for our Pals. We're going to keep trying to make them proud of us. And guess what? My Pals just found out that I've been given the Number 1 Brood Bitch award for 2011 by the Staffordshire Bull Terrier Club of America! That's because four of my babies— Killian, Annie, Pistol and Cowboy—were champions in the same year. The Club is even giving me a write-up in its magazine. Life is good!

17

Getting There

Now my Pals are talking about another trip north to visit Don's family. With Lucy, Cowboy and me in the SUV, this trip's going to be a challenge. It's a much longer ride to Wisconsin than it was to Colorado. And, of course, we'll have to stop at hotels along the way. I wonder if we'll have to sneak in one at a time so they won't know there are three of us dogs. Well, we'll do what we have to do.

While we're packing for our trip, I hear Don say we're going to stop in Kansas City to visit his daughter Sandi and his grandson Marcus and *his* two babies. So Don now has two more great grandchildren. I sure would like to have some grandpups myself. Maybe Lucy will have a litter soon. That would make everybody happy, especially me.

Now Don says we'll also be stopping in Madison. This is great news! We'll get to see Mak again. Madison is where he lives when he's not in Colorado. I remember a long time ago I went to a big, fenced-in puppy park in Madison. I was only about one year old. I ran all over the place checking everything out. Then I chased all the other dogs. I can't do that anymore, but it sure was fun. Too bad Cowboy and Lucy didn't get to go to that puppy park. But our new plans sound great. We'll be going to the big Rashke summer picnic while we're in Madison. My Pal says a lot of his relatives will be there. He has so many! I think he said fifty-four in all—so far. Can you imagine how many people will want to pet and play with us at this picnic? I wonder how my Pal keeps track of who is who.

How can anyone remember so many names? Of course, we dogs can remember everyone by their smell.

IT SEEMS TO ME THAT EVERY TIME we plan to go somewhere, somebody gets sick or has some other problem. It's no different this time. We're almost ready to go and Don has to go to the doctor. I don't know what the problem is, but I hope it's not serious. I can tell Patricia is worried. I know Don is old, but he's not *that* old. It doesn't seem fair. But like they say: "You have to be tough to get old."

Turns out, Don is okay. He just needed a change in his medicine. So now my Pals are back to making lists of things to take on the trip. Don't forget the dog food and water! With all three of us traveling in the SUV, we'll have to stop more often. I hear Don tell Patricia that he reserved a room at the Hyatt in Kansas City and they allow dogs. Yea! That was the only thing I was really worried about. We still might have to sneak in separately because there are three of us, but I know Patricia will make sure everything works out. She's happy because the hotel is in this place called the Crown Center. She likes it because that's the home of Hallmark Cards and there are lots of nice shops. Patricia *loves* nice shops!

Now my Pals arrange for some people called "castle watchers" to come over three times a week while we're gone to water our plants and check on things. It seems like you can pay people to take care of just about anything you want. I guess the castle people will also check on our new generator. Now we know we'll always have electricity in the house, even during a bad storm or hurricane. That's a relief because these Texas storms can be scary, what with all the thunder and lightning. I know from experience. I just hope nothing happens to our house while we're away. I love this place. They don't get hurricanes in Wisconsin, but I heard my Pals talking about tornadoes. I hope we don't have any of those while we're there.

THE NEXT DAY WE ALL WAKE UP very early. It's taking me a long time to get moving because of my arthritis. But even when we finally pull out of the driveway, it's still dark. My Pals talk about stopping for coffee soon and then having breakfast later. I guess that's when we'll get our treats. It looks like we'll be in the SUV for quite a while, so I'm going back to sleep now.

I don't know how long it's been, but I wake up because the car has stopped. Maybe it's treat time. Then I see a man with a badge and a gun standing next to Don's door. He's saying, "This is not the toll road. Here it's 65, not 75." Now I understand what's going on. My Pals always speed. I know that because when they're driving, they always talk about what the speed limit is on this or that highway. Then they go much faster. But I have never been in this kind of situation before—where they get CAUGHT.

This man with the badge is big and he looks pretty scary to me. He doesn't faze Don though. My Pal stays cool. My kids in the back are not very helpful with all their barking. The man wants to know why we have so many dogs with us, and if they are "pit bulls"? Maybe he thinks my Pals are taking us to a dogfight.

Patricia really comes to our rescue now. She tells the man that we are *not* pit bulls. "These are show dogs," Patricia says, like she can't believe the man could think such a thing. "They are very friendly," she goes on, "and they only bark to let us know there is a stranger here." She even tells him we are called "nanny" dogs. I'm not sure that helps much.

The highway patrol man says he's going to let Don go this time with a warning. I think that's pretty nice of him. But Patricia has some nasty things to say as we get back on the road. Believe me, when she gets upset, you don't want to be there. It's a good thing the policeman can't hear her.

We're on the road for a while when some bad smells tell my Pals it's time to let us do our business. Don pulls off the road and Patricia takes us out while Don gets gas (which is also what we had). Then we get our treats. Cowboy is pushy, as always. He just has to be first. That may be fine in the show ring, but it's not very polite at mealtime. I like it when my Pals call each of our names to come and get our treats. That way, there's no bumping and shoving. We eat our treats and my Pals have a sandwich and coffee. Then we're back on the road. I really can't wait to get wherever we're going. But at least when we stop now and then and walk around, I don't get so stiff.

Now my Pals are saying we're "halfway there." I don't know whether they mean halfway to Kansas City or halfway to the cabin. I guess, as usual, I'll just have to wait and see. With this long trip,

I'm glad they put pillows in the back of the SUV. At least when I lie on the floor back there I've got some padding.

FINALLY, I HEAR MY PALS SAY we're at the Crown Center, so I think we must be in Kansas City. We get to our hotel and it looks pretty nice. But where is the grass? I have business to do. I sure hope my Pals don't take too long to check in. Ah! Now I see it. The grass is behind the building. That's good because there are three of us and we don't want people standing around staring while we do what we have to do. Would you?

This is a very pretty hotel. The rooms are nice and big with plenty of space for all three of us to move around. It's a good thing Patricia got Cowboy to stop his marking. After we settle down, my Pals go out. I guess they're meeting with Don's daughter and grandchildren. I don't know why we couldn't go along. I'm staying right by the door to listen for them. Maybe they'll bring us a treat. They always say, "Because you were so good, we brought you something special." Of course, I won't tell them that Cowboy and Lucy have been fighting. Well, they're really just playing hard. But they're making a lot of noise. I hope no one complains or we'll be kicked out.

It's getting late and I really have to, you know, go. I hope my Pals get back soon. Maybe if I just lie down it will not be such an emergency. At home, I always stand by the door and they know what that means. Here, I don't have any way to let them know. I certainly don't want to bark. Now the door is opening. They're back! I need to let them know how urgent this is. But I don't have to worry. The first thing Patricia says is, "We better take them out. It's been a long time. Let's see, who's first?" I jump right up and grab my leash. So Cowboy and I get to go out first. Little Lucy will just have to wait. She's very impatient and I hope she doesn't start whining.

Sure enough, as soon as we're all back in the hotel room, Patricia has some special meat for us. If I heard right, it's Kansas City strip steak. It sure is good. With my nice full tummy, I guess it won't be too bad sleeping on the floor tonight. I think we need to turn in right now because we'll probably have to get up early again tomorrow. We have to make it to Madison before it gets too dark.

Just as I thought, we're up early. I'm going to catch up on my sleep in the car. I bet Patricia will do that too. All Don needs is some coffee and he's ready to go. But now we have a problem. How do we get out of Kansas City? There are so many roads. It seems to me we just keep going from one highway to another. I'm sure glad I don't have to find my way around here. It reminds me of the time Lucy and I were running around in the woods in Wisconsin and we got lost. At least here, there's no snow. I'm just going back to sleep. Let Don figure it all out.

I guess he did because we're in Iowa now. Don says this is the "Breadbasket of America." I think he must mean the "Corn Belt." That's all I can see out the window. Don says they raise enough corn here to feed half the world. But he's worried that climate changes are going to affect this area pretty soon. He says something called global warming will make it too hot and dry here to grow crops. They'll have to use irrigation. I think that means they bring water in from somewhere else, and I guess it costs a lot. Well, a lot more than rain costs. Don says right now they get rain at least every other week, but that won't last. I'm glad I'm not a human so I don't have to worry about how to fix all these big problems. But I do worry about what will happen to me and my grandpups and all the other animals if the humans don't solve these problems.

I like listening to my Pal Don while we're traveling. He's very smart and I learn a lot. If it gets to be as hot in Iowa as it gets in Texas in the summer, they'll be cooked. I'm sure glad we go to Wisconsin this time of year. We Staffies can't take much heat. I don't know how those dogs with a lot of hair can stand it. And even Killian, who can lie in the water on the top step of the pool to cool off, still has to come out into the heat sometime.

It's pretty late when we get to Madison. My Pals have made reservations for us to stay at the Marriott Hotel not far from Mak's house. We won't see my boy and his family tonight. But we'll all get together tomorrow for the picnic at the park. I can't wait.

107

18

All Together

We all sleep in a little later this morning—even my Pal Don who always gets up early. I guess we all needed to rest up from our travels so we can enjoy this big picnic today. Don takes me and Lucy out to do our business while Patricia is getting dressed. When we get back, Patricia takes Cowboy out. Now, with all our business out of the way, we dogs can finally eat our breakfast. Our Pals go downstairs to eat theirs in the hotel restaurant.

When they get back, Don says to us, "Are you all ready to go to the park?" Can't he tell from our wagging tails and our chirps that we are *so* ready? Don gathers up our stuff and says he's going to take it down to the SUV while Patricia checks us out at the desk. He says he'll be waiting for us at the front entrance. Once my Pal is gone, Patricia clips on our leashes and the four of us take the elevator down to the lobby. Patricia pays our bill and then we go outside. Sure enough, Don is waiting in the SUV. We all jump in and we're off.

It doesn't take us very long to get to this picnic park. When we pull into the parking area there are already a bunch of other cars. Don and Patricia put our leashes on. Now we can get out and really start to look around. As we walk over to the park, I can see picnic tables and people setting up grills and opening up coolers and lots of kids running around. Some people are waving at us and our Pals wave back. Then I see a part of the park that has a fence around it. Hey, I've been here before. That's the puppy park I went to when I really was just a pup. I feel right at home now!

Don and Patricia take us dogs over to the puppy park so we can ditch our leashes and stretch our legs. There are already some other dogs here, so at first our Pals keep a close eye on us. Cowboy, Lucy, and I are just sniffing around and looking at these other dogs. Then I hear a friendly chirp and guess what? It's my boy Mak! His Pals Quinn and Tia have brought him over so we can all say hi. Before you know it, the four of us dogs are chasing each other around and some other dogs we don't even know are joining in the fun. I have to stop after a while because I'm getting tired. But I never get tired of watching my kids mix it up. Then our Pals are calling us and saying it's time to eat.

Boy are they right! There are so many yummy smells coming from those grills. My mouth is starting to water. We go over with our Pals to one of the tables where some of Don's relatives are already sitting. Patricia sits down too and starts to cut up something that sure smells good. Then she puts it on three paper plates and sets them down in front of me, Lucy, and Cowboy—with a little space between us, of course. "Real Wisconsin brats," she says. Oh my, I'm in heaven. These brats are so good! As usual, Cowboy gobbles his down and finishes first. When he starts sniffing around my plate and then Lucy's, Patricia gets up, puts his leash on and takes him for a little walk so Lucy and I can finish eating in peace.

While my Pals are sitting at the table, some more of Don's relatives come over to talk. Lots of kids are running around and some of them also come over to see us dogs. At first, they seem a little afraid. But then one of them starts petting me. Then they all seem to understand that we would never hurt them and they start petting us too.

After all that running around and eating and petting, it's time for a nap. When I wake up I hear my Pals saying goodbye to some of the relatives who are leaving now. "Come up to see us," my Pals say. Then I hear Don tell Patricia, "We better get on the road too if we want to get to the cabin before dark. My Pals and Lucy, Cowboy and I head over to the parking area and climb in the SUV. Lucy and I and even Cowboy settle down pretty quick. We're all tuckered out from so much food and fun. Soon, we're all sound asleep.

I DON'T KNOW HOW LONG I've been sleeping, but I wake up when I feel the SUV slowing down and making a few turns. I look out the window and I know where we are. We're here! After Don parks the SUV, he and Patricia get out and open the back doors for us. Lucy and I jump right out. Cowboy gets out too but he doesn't know what to make of this place. He's never been here before. He was always on the show circuit whenever Lucy and I and our Pals came up. The first thing Cowboy does is walk around the car *very* slowly. He looks and then sniffs at everything. I don't know what he expects to find. Lucy and I are busy running around. Finally, Cowboy gets the idea and joins us. Right away, I remember how much cleaner the air is up here. It makes a difference to us dogs because our noses are so sensitive.

While the three of us are running around, I hear Don call out, "far enough." Of course, I know what that means: Stick around here. Thank goodness, Lucy and Cowboy follow my lead. They don't know it, but those kids could get in big trouble up here. Once we go inside the cabin, I can tell there have been other people here since last time. And there has also been a dog here. I'm sure they were all friends of my Pals. Now I'm on my way to the lower level to see if anybody was down there too. But before I can even sniff around a little bit down there, I hear Don calling me back. "Nobody goes downstairs, okay?" he says. Okay, boss.

Lucy and Cowboy and I decide to check out the back veranda. We can see that the new pier is in, but the boat isn't there. The winter storage people must be waiting for us to get here before they bring it back. I also notice that those big balls we had so much fun with last year aren't around either. I sure hope Patricia goes into town and gets some more for us. But right now—would you believe—the best thing is just to have some good, cold water. I was getting tired of that lukewarm stuff we got while we were traveling.

After we unpack and settle in, we head down to the pier. My Pals put a leash on Cowboy. They just want to make sure he knows what *not* to do before they let him roam around. Lucy and I already know the rules, even though I try to break them once in a while. But Cowboy still has a lot to learn about this neck of the woods.

When we get down to the lake, I can see that the water is higher than last year. This makes everyone happy, especially Don. He's been worried that we wouldn't be able to get the boat up to the pier if the water level didn't rise over the winter. I guess now they can bring the boat over. I hope Don will be able to climb back up all these steps to the cabin. It's hard for me, so I know it must be hard for him. At least he has a railing to hold onto. That thing's too high to help me. It's very tiring to jump up all those stairs, one-by-one. Patricia says she's thinking of getting me a harness so she can give me a little pull without hurting my neck. I know what a harness is. We used to wear them when Don took us out for a run alongside his golf cart back in Texas. Maybe Patricia should get a harness for each of us dogs. Then we could jog alongside the ATV and Don wouldn't have to worry about us running off into the woods. I wish I could talk to Patricia about this idea of mine.

I just love the fresh air up here. It makes me feel younger—like I can still run really fast and do just about anything. One time I heard my Pals talking and they said they *feel* like they can still do all the things they did as young people, even if they really can't. I guess I'm the same way. Like when we are all chasing a ball. I'm very competitive. I don't want anyone else to have that ball. I still *think* I can beat Lucy or Cowboy or anyone else when we play keep-away, even if I really can't.

Patricia's grandson Josh is coming to visit us today. That means we'll have to stay home while they go out to "golf." I don't know what's so special about this "golf," but they sure like it. I've watched the golf on TV with my Pals and it looks pretty boring. Everyone is just standing around or walking. Now I like walking, but if I were out there with all the grass and trees around me, I think I'd be doing a little running too. I know Lucy and Cowboy sure would.

Turns out, Don is staying home with us. Maybe he doesn't like golf anymore. Then I hear him say to Josh, "Oh, I just go with Patricia to keep her company." I guess Josh can keep Patricia company today.

I REALLY LIKE IT MUCH BETTER when we do things together. Like when we go shopping in the town that has all those benches and people walking around. That's where we're headed now. I hear my Pals say the name of this town. It's that funny Indian name—Minocqua. I think I went to see the doctor there when I was pregnant.

When we get into town, Don sits on a bench with us while Patricia goes shopping. It's fun because people always come over and talk to us. They all say how pretty we are. Some even pet us, which I really like. But some people seem afraid. They ask Don if we bite and he

Me, Lucy, and Cowboy relaxing with our Pal at the cabin.

says, "Only if they are defending me." The ladies always like this story and start petting me after that. I'm probably the easiest for strangers to pet. Cowboy is so friendly he almost knocks people over when he jumps up to get their attention. Of course, he would never bite anyone. But strangers don't know that, do they?

We've been waiting near this bench for a long time. Patricia must be buying lots of things. Finally, Don grabs our leashes and says, "Let's go get some ice cream." Yes! Lucy and I share a dish. Of course, Cowboy has to have his own dish. He'd never share. Yumm. This is soooo good. When we're finished, Don holds out the cone he bought for himself and lets us lick all the ice cream that's left. The people walking by think that's really cute. We'd do it again if they would buy us another ice cream cone.

At last, Patricia comes over to our bench and, sure enough, she has lots of packages. When we get back to the cabin, she gives us each a new toy. I get mad when Cowboy and Lucy gang up on me and try to take away my toy. I have to stand my ground and remind them who I am. My "mean" growl does the trick. It says: Leave my toy alone. Don't mess with your mama.

I LIKE IT NOW THAT WE'RE ALL BACK sleeping together in my Pals' bedroom. When we first got up here, Cowboy was always making noises at night and checking my Pals' bed to make sure they were still there. So we had to put him in a kennel by himself in the living room at night just so the rest of us could get some sleep. Of course, he got lonely out there all by himself. In the middle of the night, he'd start crying and wake everyone up. After this went on for a while, we decided to let him come back in the bedroom. He seems to have learned his lesson. And everyone's sleeping much better now that we're all back together. Cowboy insists on sleeping next to Lucy. I wonder if there's anything going on between those two?

This morning, after breakfast, all three of us go with Don out to the garage. He wants to check all his "equipment." He sure has a lot of stuff. Besides the four-wheel-drive ATV, there's a snowmobile, a wagon, and a big tractor. My Pal tells us the tractor belongs to his son Richie. He's the one who takes care of the place when we're not here. We dogs sniff around some more and find a lawn mower, some tools, and all kinds of other things—batteries and a bunch of small machines that hook up to the tractor. I don't know how Don remembers what to do with all these things. Sometimes he gets mad when he's trying to make something work. Then he hollers a lot and scares us all.

I guess the lake water is still low. I hear Don talking about how hard it will be to get the boat in and out. He gives us his "climate change" speech again. He says the weather is changing all over. Some parts of the country are very dry and there are forest fires. In other places the snow is melting and the rivers overflow. Of course, I know about snow. But rivers and fires I can't understand, unless he's talking about the fireplace. That's a fire I like, especially when it's cold outside. But all these other climate changes worry me.

19

Adventure Land

We're back in Texas now. But I wonder for how long. Don says we can think about doing some *serious* traveling now that we're all together. But before we can really start planning another trip, Cowboy has some serious business of his own to attend to. And I don't mean pooping. The folks in Georgia say their females will be in heat soon. They need Cowboy to come visit and "do his thing."

My Pals call our critter sitters, Tolef and Carol, and arrange for them to stay with me and Lucy for three days. Then Don, Patricia, and Cowboy head off to Georgia. I guess everything goes smoothly because three days later they're all back and everyone seems happy. Now we can begin our trip planning. I like these long bye-byes. We always get good treats, and the special food my Pals give us along the way is always delicious. Plus, we get to explore lots of different places and sniff out all kinds of new smells. Every day is a holiday.

Don says the plan is to head west and north up into the Texas Panhandle, then go west through New Mexico and into Arizona. There we'll see the Grand Canyon. Yea! I guess. I have to admit I'm completely over my head here. I have no idea what these panhandle and canyon places are, but they sound like fun.

We're taking the motor home this time because my Pals think we might have to "camp out" in some places. I just hope we can also stay in some nice hotels along the way. Lucy, Cowboy and I are pretty experienced travelers by now, so it isn't long before we're on the road and headed for this Grand Canyon. It takes us quite a while to get there, but boy is it worth it. This Grand Canyon is awesome! It's also very deep. I won't let my Pals take me too close to the edge because I might fall in. I think they realize that all three of us are a little

This Grand Canyon is huge and deep...and a little scary.

I feel much safer on the overlook with a fence.

nervous near this Grand Canyon. They take us over to a lookout area with fences. That feels safer. We all just stand there and stare down into this great big hole. I hear Don say to Patricia: "How would you like to be heading west and come to this, not knowing how far it goes either way?" Well, I was thinking the same thing. I wonder how long it will take us to get around this giant hole?

Don pulls out one of his maps now and starts to study it. I know from experience that these maps are important for travelers like us so we know where we're going. After Don studies, we get back into the motor home. It only takes us until dinnertime to get to the end of the canyon where we stop for the night. We all sit outside the motor home and eat our dinner. When it starts getting dark, we go inside and lock the door. I'm really sleepy tonight. It must be all this nice, fresh, cool air. Our three kennels are lined up side-by-side and in we go for the night. Then the lights go off. Then I drift off. I feel very safe. I know Don will be up making coffee in the morning and then he'll take us out one at a time while Patricia makes breakfast. It's good to have a routine you can count on, especially when you're traveling.

In the morning, after breakfast, we head west again like those early settlers who finally found a way around this Grand Canyon. Pretty soon, Don says we're crossing into Nevada. I think this Nevada must also be a state like Arizona and New Mexico and Texas. Wow, we've been in four states already.

We aren't in Nevada very long before we come to a big, big wall that Don says is holding back a lot of water. I sure hope it doesn't break while we're here. Don says this is the Hoover Dam. It's named after one of our presidents. But it used to be called Boulder Dam because it holds back water from the Boulder River. It also makes electricity for thousands of homes and businesses. That's amazing. I can't wait to see how they get electricity from water. But Don is explaining it all to Patricia so I listen too.

My Pal says there are these big generators deep down inside this dam. He says that this big wall (the dam) is holding back trillions of gallons of water and only lets enough through to turn the generators that make the electricity. Usually, Patricia is not interested in these kinds of details. But this thing is so big that she wants to know how they could build it while the river was flowing through. Then she's wondering how much pressure is on that wall, which is curved

Don and Patricia are going down inside the Hoover Dam.

I'd be afraid to do that.

against the water. And what if it leaks? I'd like to know about some of these things too, especially the leaks.

It turns out that people, but not dogs, can get on an elevator and go down where the generators are. My Pals decide to take the tour. Don parks the motor home and cracks a window for us. Lucy, Cowboy and I just stretch out and rest up for our next adventure. My Pals aren't gone too long, and when they get back they can't stop talking about the tour. How they went down five hundred feet in the elevator to the generator room. How big the generator is, I can't even imagine. I think I would be afraid to go down so deep. Maybe it's better that they don't allow dogs on that tour.

From here we head to Las Vegas. Thank goodness it isn't very far because we're all starting to get hungry. It's nighttime when we get there and it's a beautiful sight with all those lights. As usual, we have to drive around a while to find a hotel that takes dogs. After we eat, Don and Patricia go to another part of the hotel that's for "gambling." We dogs are not allowed over there, so I don't know what goes on. It seems like they're gone for a long time. But we don't mind because it's a nice room and we can jump up on the bed and relax.

Las Vegas is quite a sight at night.

After a while Don comes back to check on us and take us outside—one at a time—to do our business. While my Pal and I are out, he tells me that Patricia won three hundred dollars. Wow! That sounds like a lot. I guess this "gambling" must be a good way to make money. Patricia must still be making money over there. Maybe Don came back because he can't make any money. After we've all done our business, my Pal settles us down in the room and leaves again. I think he's going back to the gambling to help Patricia make more money. It's pretty late at night when both our Pals come back. Patricia doesn't show us any money, but she gives us the most delicious meat treats. Thank goodness these hotels have "doggie bags." You can see why we like traveling.

TODAY DON'S LOOKING AT A MAGAZINE that tells about all the shows they have in this Las Vegas place. He says there are so many shows, it's the only way to decide which ones they want to go to. Of course, we can't go with them. I mean, these are not *dog* shows. So here's the drill. They take us out right before they leave and then right after they come back from their show. But hey, it's not too bad. They always come back with a treat. I think they feel guilty because they've left us for so long. If that means a treat, I'm sure not going to tell them any different.

On our second day here, there's a loud knock on our hotel door. It's some kind of manager. He tells Don there is a complaint about us dogs. Don asks: "What kind of complaint? It certainly can't be for barking." Well, of course not. We don't bark. The manager explains that the lady staying next door says she is afraid of the "big one." That means Cowboy. Don asks the manager if Cowboy got too close to her or if he tried to jump on her or something. The manager says no, she is just afraid.

Don tries to tell him about us Staffies and our background. You know, how gentle we are. How we love babies and children. How we wouldn't hurt anyone. But this doesn't do any good. So finally, Don asks if they could move us to another room. The manager seems surprised.

"Hey," he says, "you wouldn't mind?"

"Heck no," Don says. "Let's just do it."

Everyone's happy except Patricia. She says it always falls on her to do all the work. She'll have to pack everything up and move everyone and all our stuff to another room. She says it's a great inconvenience.

"Oh, no," the manager says, "I'll send someone up to help you get everything together and move it to the new room."

I think that's pretty nice. And Patricia's feeling a little better now. Don says these hotels will do almost anything to please us because they want our money. I'll have to think about this. We dogs are always trying to please our Pals too. But we don't want their money. We just want to make them happy. Maybe people aren't like us.

Now we're in a different room on a different floor. I think it's even nicer than the other one. The manager has put us on the level that has special food and other stuff for the guests. Don says it's called the "concierge floor." It's for special guests and it also has a valet to help them. I'll have to see if I can figure out what this "valet" is. After we settle in, my Pals say they're going to another room on our floor that serves food and drinks. Oh boy! When they come back they bring us the greatest treats. My mouth starts watering when I hear Patricia say, "They'll love this filet of steak." Boy, is she right. Real meat is a lot better than those treats that come in bags from the grocery store. As far as I'm concerned, we can stay here for the rest of our vacation.

AFTER FOUR DAYS OF ALL THESE NICE THINGS, we're getting ready to travel again. This time, Don says, we're going to backtrack to New Mexico. We already drove through there, but now we'll stop in Albuquerque where my Pals want to look at some southwestern art. That sounds like fun. When we finally get there, Don parks the motor home in a shady place near some grass and we all get out. There are lots of people and kids and dogs around. Don buys us each some ice cream. Yum! It's cold and it slides around a lot in my dish, but it tastes so good! Of course, as usual, Cowboy gobbles his up and comes over for whatever I have left. I just move to the side and let him have it—this time. I think he knows by now that he can only push me so far before I play Mom again and give him a piece of my mind.

Albuquerque sure is a different kind of city. Everything is so pretty and the buildings all look, as Don says, "very Spanish." There are lots of shady places with pools of water, and the streets are made out of what Patricia calls "cobblestone." She goes off to explore some of the art galleries and shops and we hang out with Don in one of these nice, shady parks. The three of us dogs don't give our Pal any trouble. We've been taught to behave very well in public—and usually we do. We're all used to the big shows with lots of people and dogs. The only time Don has to be careful here in Albuquerque is if another dog comes around. He has to hold onto our leashes because we just want to go over and play with a new friend.

After Patricia has checked out the shops, she comes back to get us and takes us over to one of the shops. The owner brings out a vase for Don to look at. It's big and pretty and my Pals decide to buy it. The store wraps it up real good and soon we're off again.

THIS TIME WE'RE HEADING FOR A TOWN called Taos. It's in New Mexico too, but up north in the mountains. I just found out that there's a whole country called Mexico down south of us. I wonder why they don't call that one Old Mexico? I guess I'll never know.

In Taos, we stay at a condominium that belongs to one of Patricia's friends. My Pal says she has known this lady for twenty-five years and she's always been very generous to her. Wow! I sure hope I can keep my friends that long. But that would be, oops, one hundred and seventy-five dog years. No way, José! Even my Pals can't live that long.

After we get settled in the condo, we all take a hike up the mountain trail. Even Don goes. I can run up this hill faster than my Pals. But, of course, Lucy and Cowboy beat us all. We have to keep an eye on Cowboy when he's not on his leash because he hasn't had all the training that Lucy and I got from our Pals. Except for the time Cowboy and I went to Europe with our Pals, he was always with his handler when he was out on the show circuit. Not like Lucy and me. When we were showing, we were always with Don and Patricia. After we won our ribbons in the ring, we'd go to all kinds of places with our Pals and we learned to behave.

This hike is taking us alongside a stream. Don says: "You know, there must be a mountain spring creating this stream. I bet the water is so pure and cold they could bottle and sell it like the ads that say 'pure, clean, spring water.'" I'm so thirsty from all this walking that I just have to go over for a drink. Don's right. This water sure is cold. This little stream is running pretty fast. And it's so clear you can see the rocks on the bottom. Lucy and Cowboy see me and, of course, they come over for a drink too. My Pals brought a bottle of water for themselves. I think they're missing out. This is the best water I have ever tasted.

Don says this mountain is 6,000 feet above sea level. I wonder how they measure such a high mountain? Maybe they fly over in an airplane or somebody walks to the top and counts the steps. Now we are almost up to the level that skiers go. There's a lodge up here with a restaurant, so I know we're going to get something good to eat. Does it seem like I'm always thinking of food? I have to. It's bred into me. Eat, play, nap. Repeat.

Up at this level, there's also a ski trail for beginners. Of course, Lucy, Cowboy and I could run down this slope just as fast as a beginning skier. But going up, Patricia says, the skiers use a lift, like they did when we visited Mak and his family in Colorado. Patricia says if it were winter now there would be about four feet of snow on the ground up here. I wouldn't be able to run up or down this mountain in snow that deep. I would just stay at the condo and watch the skiers ride the lift up and ski down.

So what's next?

20

Rocky Mountain High

It looks like we'll be staying in the motor home from now on. There aren't many hotels on this part of the trip. Don says we'll be traveling in the "Rocky Mountains." These mountains must be special because he says we will have beautiful sights on our way north through Colorado.

As we're driving, Don and Patricia are talking about what would be a good route through the "Rockies." Then Patricia says after we leave Denver we should go to the Yellowstone National Park to see "Old Faithful." She says we shouldn't miss it. It was the first geyser in the park to be named. And it's the most predictable. I wonder what this "geyser" thing does all the time that makes people want to see it? I wonder if it's as big as the Grand Canyon?

We've really had to work on training Cowboy during our trip. He has to learn not to crowd our Pal Don while he's driving. And he needs to know that if he runs around too much, he'll be put in his kennel for a timeout. And there's another issue to be settled. While we're on the road, Lucy and I are used to lying down near Patricia's feet. This is *our* spot and I don't intend to let Cowboy push me away. After all, Lucy and I were here first. I let Cowboy know he has only two choices. He can go up on the couch or he can lie down on the carpeted floor. He tries the floor first, but if he's lying there he gets in Patricia's way when she tries to go over to the kitchen area. Once Patricia puts a blanket on the couch, everything is fine. Cowboy jumps right up and settles in. Sometimes, this motor home travel can be a challenge.

Once we have the *inside* rules set, we need to have a plan to get everyone outside safely. It's not so simple, especially when Don's busy taking care of something else and can't help. Patricia has to put all three of us on our leashes. Then, while keeping hold of the leashes, she needs to open the door of the motor home. Then she has to get us out one by one. It's pretty complicated. For starters, who should go first? We all know who *wants* to go first. Cowboy, of course. I think it will be easier if Patricia puts the leash on Cowboy and then puts him in his kennel. Then she can get Lucy and me ready to go out. Cowboy doesn't really mind going into his kennel. He's done it so many times at dog shows. Sure enough, I hear Patricia saying to herself, I think I should put Cowboy in his kennel before I open the door. Maybe she read my mind. I've heard there are people who can do that.

The new "exit" plan works much better and we finally manage to get everyone outside. The air up here in these mountains is wonderful. Patricia says the air is "thin" up here. I wonder what that means? Is there "fat" air? I don't notice any real difference. Except I see that Don can't walk very far up here before he says he needs to sit down and "catch his breath." His mouth is open, his tongue is out a little, and he's breathing fast. I think that means he's "panting." Just like we dogs do.

After a short walk around, we're back on the road. This motor home is so smooth, it almost puts you to sleep. Pretty soon we come to a narrow strip in the mountain and the road starts to get steeper. Don must be putting the motor in a lower gear because we all jerk forward. He says we're now at 12,000 feet. I think that's the highest I've ever been, even higher than when we were in Colorado. Of course, when I was up in airplanes—coming here to America, going to New York, and then our trip to Europe—I was much higher than these mountains.

I go up to the front window and look out on Patricia's side. There's lots of snow. It looks just like winter in Wisconsin. Then I go over to the window on the other side behind Don and I can see another hill (I mean mountain) that is so high I can't even see the bottom of it. Back at the front window I'm trying to see the top of this mountain. Now Lucy comes over and puts her nose up against the window to see this big mountain too. Of course, Cowboy senses something interesting is going on and he comes over to check it out. Now all three of us are crowding into the front of the motor home while Don is trying to drive up this steep hill. We're not here very long before Patricia comes up front. She gives us her serious "No" and points to the back of the motor home. The three of us don't waste any time heading to the back. We know that tone. It means we're really going to "get it" if we don't do what we're told.

NOW DON SAYS WE'RE HEADED toward Yellowstone National Park. It's in the state of Wyoming, but he says the park goes all the way into Montana. We sure have been in a lot of states on this trip. I'll bet you this "Old Faithful" geyser at the park will be something to see. Don was right when he told us there was so much beauty out here.

It seems to me there is no end to these mountains. We're now camping for the third day and it's cooler here. Don says you've got to watch out for bears, especially when you're eating outside. They can smell the food and will come over to check it out. My Pal says these bears are called either Grizzly or Brown bears. They are big and can run faster than a person. Well, that's not going to scare *us*. My ancestors were bear hunters and I know we are faster than those critters. We would protect our Pals. It's just too bad we can't tell them that. But they do know that whenever we hear a noise, our ears perk up and we are ready for anything. So bears beware.

"Well, here it is," Don says. "Buffalo Bill Cody's Yellowstone Country."

It's almost dark when we finally get to the camping area at Yellowstone. Coming into a big park like this is quite a change from where we camped on the way here. There are lots of campers. There's a building with all kinds of shops, restaurants and tour guides. Not exactly the "wilderness."

Once we get settled in, Patricia says, she'll take us for a little walk to do our business. Right now, she's in and out of the motor home trying to get things organized. Don's busy starting up the grill outside. And me…well, I can see that there's too much going on all at the same time. No one's really paying attention. That usually means trouble.

Sure enough, before Patricia can get a leash on Cowboy, he jumps out the door and off he goes into the dark. Right away, Don starts calling for him. Then Patricia calls. There's no answer and no Cowboy. Other campers around us come over to see what's going on. They can't help, of course, but it's nice that they care. I think I can just barely see Cowboy way over on a hill. It looks like he's chasing something. It could be anything. I know there are all kinds of animals up here. I also know that he better turn around and come back. He may think he's a hunter, but I know he'll get lost and maybe get hurt. Remember that awful sandstorm in Belgium?

Patricia puts a leash on me and we start walking in the direction that Cowboy ran. We walk for a long time—up and down small hills and across little creeks. We stop at caves and call for him. I give our special chirp. No Cowboy. It's getting really dark now. Patricia turns on her flashlight so we can keep looking. I'm starting to wonder if we'll be able to find our way back to the campsite. Patricia's thinking the same thing. She sits down on a rock, gets out her cell phone, and calls Don. He tells her to use the phone's GPS map and dial up our present location. Then he says to dial up "Old Faithful" and that will lead us back to the park.

But Cowboy is lost in the wilderness! What should we do about him? Don says just come back to camp and we'll figure something out.

When we get back, my Pals start up the motor home so they can turn on the headlights. Maybe Cowboy will see them and find his way back. The four of us have dinner outside, with Lucy and me in the little corral as usual. Maybe Cowboy will smell our dinner or hear us. But there's no sign of him. I'm getting worried. It's not like at home where there are houses nearby and lots of people. Don starts tooting the small horn on the motor home, not the big honker because he doesn't want to disturb the other campers. I know he's hoping he might get Cowboy's attention. Between honks, there's only silence. Now Lucy and I are scared because we know our Pals are scared.

We stay outside for a long time watching for Cowboy and hoping he'll come back. My Pals leave the lights on to discourage any animals from coming into our little camp. Finally, Don says he's going to take a lantern and head out the way Cowboy went. Patricia says, "No! I was out there. It's endless." My Pals seem to think the Forest Service might be able to help, but not until daylight. It's really late now. They decide the only thing we can do is get some sleep. Patricia, Lucy and I stretch out on the couch. Don sleeps up front in the driver's seat. No one sleeps very well.

In the morning Don is up first. He makes coffee and then takes Lucy and me outside. While we're eating breakfast, Patricia's cell phone rings. We hear her say, "Where? In Madison?" She talks for a while. Then she sets her phone on the table. She tells us that the call was from a drugstore in the nearby town of Madison, Wyoming. Patricia says a State Trooper picked Cowboy up and drove him over there. The trooper thought that because my boy had a collar and tags, he might also have an embedded recovery chip. Of course he does. We all have these chips and they don't bother us at all. The veterinarian puts them in and they register all our information with the American Kennel Club, including phone numbers and where we live and who our Pals are. Patricia starts crying as she's telling us all this. Lucy and I aren't sure what to think. But then we see that she's "happy crying" because Cowboy is safe.

It doesn't take us long to drive over to Madison. It's just on the other side of the park. We pull up at the drugstore and there's Cowboy. He runs up to say hello as if nothing happened. He sure is hungry though. Patricia fixes him a nice meal and he digs right in. I bet he doesn't even realize *he* could have been some animal's dinner last night. But Patricia isn't even mad at him. In fact, she seems to love Cowboy even more after he was a bad dog and ran off and scared us all. I guess I shouldn't be jealous. My Pals always make sure Lucy and I get plenty of love and petting too. And I can tell they feel real bad whenever they see my arthritis flaring up. I guess our Pals just love us in different ways at different times.

WHEN COWBOY HAS FINISHED EATING, he and Don have a serious chat. Well, Don does the talking and Cowboy *looks* like he's paying attention.

"Cowboy," Don says sternly, "this is the second time you've charged off on your own. Once in Europe and then last night. That's two strikes. One more strike and you are OUT. No more traveling. You'll stay in a kennel at home."

Cowboy sits looking up at my Pal for a long minute. Then he walks closer to Don, sits down at his feet, and stares up with that real sad look he can put on. No one can resist it, not even Don. All is forgiven.

Now that my boy is back safe and sound from *his* adventures, we can continue *ours*. We pile into the motor home and head back to Yellowstone. Finally, we get to see what we came for. To get to the geyser, we have to drive through the Big Horn Mountains. All of a sudden, there it is—Old Faithful—like a giant fountain shooting jets of water and steam way up in the air. Awesome. Then, just as quickly, there's nothing.

Now you see it. Now you don't. This Old Faithful geyser is really something.

We park the motor home in the lot and head over to where we saw the geyser spurting. Don says it's dangerous to get too close because the geyser's very hot. That's why they have a fence around it. We join a lot of people just standing around waiting. Then, whoosh! Here it goes again. It's amazing and a little scary. The Park Service guy tells us that Old Faithful has been doing this for years and years. He says scientists studied the geyser and found that its "eruption schedule" is very predictable. That's why they call it Old Faithful. He says the U.S. government made all this area a National Forest and Park. It stretches over more than two million acres across three states. And it's "protected land." That means no hunting. I'm really happy to be learning all these new things about America.

Tonight, while we're having our dinner outside the motor home, Don says we should go over to the Grand Teton Mountain Range. He says it's a little south of where we are now, but it's something we should see as long as we're so close. Then, he says, we'll come back through Yellowstone and head west to pick up the Washington-Oregon Trail and take it down into California. I'm game.

AFTER WE BACKTRACK A LITTLE to see the Tetons, our plan now is to head northwest through the mountains of Montana. Then we'll cross into Idaho and over to Washington state. Patricia is wondering why we don't just go straight to California. But Don really wants us to see what he calls the "Pacific Northwest." But first, he says, we have to catch I-90 in Montana. Come on now! Catch I-90? I've traveled a lot and I know that I-90 is a highway. You can't catch a big, heavy highway. Sometimes I simply don't understand "people talk." Maybe they say these things just to confuse me. Whatever.

It's really beautiful up here in the mountains. Don says they're part of a national forest too. There are a lot of trees, that's for sure. And I bet there are a lot of squirrels too. But we're traveling too fast to see them. I wish we could stop and get out and chase a few. Pretty soon we *will* have to stop because it's getting dark. I wonder if we'll park the motor home in the middle of the forest? I think this would be a big mistake. Too scary.

Patricia's on her phone now. When she gets off she says we'll be staying in the Coeur D'Alene area of Idaho. She just made reservations at the Whidbey Inn in the old town of Coupeville. We get there pretty quick. Patricia takes us dogs out to do our business while Don goes in to check on our room.

I'm sniffing around in this nice clean air when I pick up some new smells. They seem to be coming from over there in the woods. I wish Patricia would take me off this leash. Don always used to let us run free. But after our scare with Cowboy, I know what he would say: "Yeah, sure! So you can go out and get killed." Of course he's right, but I still like the excitement of running around and exploring things on my own. This great big clearing in front of the inn with no roads would be perfect. Now Don comes back outside and I watch him. I think he may be looking around for a place to let us run. He takes the leashes from Patricia, who heads over to the inn. Don checks to see that our collars are on good. Then he takes off our leashes.

Fun! Fun! Fun! All three of us are running as fast as we can across this clearing. It feels so good to stretch our legs after being cooped up in the motor home for so long. We all make a quick turn together. Then we split up and run in different directions. Even from a distance I can tell Don's upset. Now Patricia comes out of the inn and is talking to Don. While I'm watching them to see how angry Patricia is, I notice that Lucy's not around. I go over to my Pals and begin to whimper. At first, they don't pay any attention to me. Then Cowboy comes over and the two of us start barking and circling around our Pals. They figure out pretty quick why Cowboy and I are upset.

Oh my! Is Patricia mad! Another dog lost in the woods. And this time it's Lucy. I can't repeat all the things she says, but she blames Don for losing "her" dog. I'm surprised but Don stays pretty calm. "Instead of arguing about whose fault this is," he says, "let's make a plan to go out there and look for her."

Don's right when he says we all can't just head out in different directions. We'll get lost and that won't help poor Lucy. "We have to find some paint," he says, heading toward the inn. When he comes back out, he's with the manager. They're carrying two paint buckets and two brushes. Here's the plan, I think. Don and Patricia will each take a bucket and a brush. As they walk into the woods, they'll put paint marks on the trees about every twenty feet. That way, when they want to come back, they'll just follow the paint marks. My Pal is so smart! Before they start walking, they take our kennels out of the motor home and set them on the grass. Then they put Cowboy and me inside. My Pals seem to think that we can help. If we are chirping and barking, Lucy might hear us and come out of the forest. Cowboy and I are pretty scared being locked in our kennels outside in this strange place. Sure, we can make some noise for Lucy. But we feel pretty exposed out here. However, my Pals are thinking about Lucy, not about me and Cowboy.

It's getting late now and the woods are almost dark. I watch my Pals head out calling for Lucy as they go deeper into the forest. After a while, they both come back looking very discouraged. There's no sign of Lucy and they can't see very far into the woods because it's getting so dark. Then Don gets another idea. He'll go out again with a flashlight and me on a leash. Patricia says that's dangerous and Don agrees. But with me along, he says, at least there's a chance that I can chirp or bark and Lucy will hear me.

Don and I start walking into the dark woods. I'm scared but I'm going to do everything I can to help. I start chirping every now and then but there's no reply. We go in about one hundred yards and then…there's Lucy. She's sitting in a little clearing looking at us as if to say: I was just on my way home. What's the problem? Don and I can't really get mad at her. We're just so happy we found our little girl.

The next morning we return all the search and rescue "equipment" to the hotel manager. He's happy to hear that Lucy is safe. I know Don feels responsible for her running off and all the trouble and worry it caused. But he also likes to give us some off-leash running exercise. I bet we don't get any more of that until we're back home in Texas. And that will be a long time.

BUT WHAT DO I KNOW? We're driving along on I-90 again headed west for this Washington state place. My Pals are talking, but I'm not paying much attention. Then Don says to Patricia, "You know, we should just turn around here while we're on a major east-west highway. Then we can pick up a highway heading south to Texas. Right away, Patricia agrees. She's just hoping there are no more "incidents." I'm not thinking about incidents, I'm thinking how far we have to travel. It will take us at least three days and that's a long time to be cooped up in a motor home. But at least we're heading home.

By the end of the day, we've left Montana and crossed into South Dakota. We leave I-90 and spend the night in a Wal-Mart parking lot. In the morning, Don says the plan is to head south for a while through South Dakota's Black Hills. As long as we're passing through, he says, we might as well "see what there is to see." Turns out there's a lot. One of the most popular sites in the Black Hills National Forest is Mount Rushmore. Don says they have the heads of four presidents carved right into the mountain. I don't really understand what this means until we actually get there. We pull into the parking area and Patricia puts our leashes on. Then we get out and start to sniff and look around. At first, all I can see is a lot of people far away, and they're all looking up. Then I look up too and see them—these really, really, really big heads. And they're carved right into the mountain, just like Don said. Too bad for us, they only allow "service dogs" to get closer to the memorial. Not regular dogs like us.

Even from a distance, the carvings of the presidents are amazing.

My Pals take turns staying with us so each of them can see the carvings better. For anyone who doesn't know, the guide at the memorial tells visitors who the four presidents on the mountain are— from left to right there's George Washington, Thomas Jefferson, Theodore Roosevelt and Abraham Lincoln. Don says that's a pretty good group of guys.

Now we're heading east again toward Sioux Falls. Don says we'll be passing through the "Badlands." That sounds scary but, when we get there, it isn't. The Badlands National Park is beautiful. The road we're on runs through big stretches of prairie with lots of cool looking mountains rising in the distance. I wish we could get out and explore. But we're on a mission—to get home.

Don says we're going to pick up I-90 again all the way to Sioux Falls and into Minnesota. We'll stay on I-90 through southern Minnesota until we hit I-35 South. Then, Don says, it's a straight shot south through Iowa, Missouri, Kansas, Oklahoma and, finally, Texas. And all the way to Dallas. Then Don says we'll cut over to I-45 and we'll be on our way home.

I have to say, my mind's kind of a blur passing through all these states. We only stop for meals and potty breaks and overnight rests. Traveling can be fun, but home is where we want to be now.

21

Texas at Last

We finally pull into our own driveway. Home at last. Of course, Cowboy is the first one to jump out. It doesn't matter. None of us need leashes this time. Cowboy runs around checking everything—inside and out. I think he's sniffing for signs that someone else has been in our house while we were gone. Lucy and I do the same thing, but we're not in such a big rush. It's so good to be home. We can romp around in our big backyard. We can lie down in all our favorite napping places.

Don has lots of things to check out too. He says he's going to the post office to pick up the mail. All three of us stare up at him, silently begging. "Can we go too?" I know from experience that this triple stare usually works. Don says, "Yes, let's go bye-bye!" and opens the front door. We all run out and wait for him at the garage. You wouldn't think we'd be so excited about taking another car ride. But somehow we know it's just a short one. Then we'll be coming back home. Don opens the car door and we all jump in. You know, it doesn't take much to make us happy.

We wait in the car while our Pal goes into the post office. When he comes out, he's carrying a great big box. It must be all our mail. Back home, he sits down at the table and starts to dig into the box. "This will take a while to sort through," he says to Patricia. Then we hear Don say, "Wow!" Our six ears perk up. He calls Patricia over to take a look.

Don holds up some kind of big metal coin. He calls it a medallion. He's showing Patricia where it says "American Kennel Club" around the edge. And in the middle are the words "Grand Champion" and "GCH Bronze Level." It turns out that while we were on the road, the AKC made a special award for Champions who earn a standing in the top twenty leaders. There's a bronze, a silver, and, at the top, a gold medallion.

This is wonderful news for Cowboy. I'm so excited. And so are my Pals, of course. Since he's not competing any more, it's probably the highest honor he'll get. I'm very proud of my boy. Cowboy is really special. Physically, he's a perfect example of the male of our breed. But he's also very sensitive. Whenever Patricia bawls him out for doing something he shouldn't, he jumps on the couch and lies there with his head on the cushion. Then he looks up at her with his big, brown eyes that say, "I'm *so* sorry, I'll never do that again." As you can tell, Cowboy is also very smart. Patricia can never stay mad at him for long.

Right now, however, Cowboy couldn't care less about his latest honor. He's snoozing on the sofa, just glad to be home. But it looks like Patricia has other ideas. A couple of days later I hear her talking to Don. "You know," she says, "now that our three champions are all retired, we should get some glamour photos made while they're still in their prime." Uh oh.

About a week later, Patricia takes us over to our local groomer— Bed, Bath and Biscuit—where we all (except Patricia, of course) get a shampoo and a blow-dry. We also get our nails done. We dogs are all ready to go home but Patricia says, "Not so fast." It turns out that BB&B has hired a professional photographer to take photos of all its clients and it will use them in a video. Patricia will get free proofs and she can have copies of any photos she likes. The photographer and his wife—who is also his assistant—are already here. The wife takes our leashes and tells us what wonderful dogs we are. Hmm. This could be fun.

A few feet in front of us, her husband the photographer guy is setting up his camera on top of three sticks called a tripod. Pretty soon, the oohing and ahing about how great we dogs are has turned into orders. Jump up here on this cushion. Sit real still. Move closer together. Hold your head up. Look straight ahead. Smile.

We show dogs love to have our pictures taken...

But sometimes it can take a while...

To get it just perfect. From left: me, Cowboy, and Lucy.

Photos by James D. Bass, Le' Image/Glamour Pets

By now, Cowboy, Lucy, and I are getting a little restless. I mean, it's not like we're in the show ring competing for a ribbon. But we must be doing something right because I can hear the camera clicking away. The photographer's wife keeps moving us around, holding up her hands to get us to look the right way, telling us to sit or stand up or lie down. Boy, this photo stuff sure is tiring. I guess the photographer finally gets enough shots that he thinks are good. At last we can get down from our perches and go home and eat the Frosty Paws that Patricia gives us for being such good dogs.

MY PALS HAVE DECIDED THAT NOW'S THE TIME to try breeding Lucy and Cowboy again. We'll all be going up to the cabin in Wisconsin for the summer. My Pals want to do the breeding here in Texas and then let Lucy deliver her pups up north. I agree. That's where I had my first babies—Killian, Mak and, of course, Lucy. It's a wonderful place for "younguns" to come into the world.

In early April, my Pals try to get Cowboy and Lucy together here at the house. But I guess my two kids just can't work things out the "natural" way. So they take Lucy and Cowboy to our vet. If I understand it right, he says artificial insemi-something is the way to go. He knows we'll be up north for the delivery. The babies have to grow inside Lucy for about sixty to sixty-three days before they're ready to come out. Our vet here wants to be able to tell the vet up in Wisconsin exactly when the babies started to grow inside Lucy. That way, he can set up a firm delivery date. Her pups will have to be born by what they call a C-section. My little girl is just too small for a natural delivery. I know all about C-sections. They're no fun, but we'll do whatever is best for Lucy and her puppies. So what happens is—the vet takes some sperm from Cowboy and injects it into Lucy. That's all I know.

I guess the artificial stuff went okay. When Lucy and Cowboy get home from the vet, you'd think they just came back from a nice walk. My Pals, on the other hand, seem pretty excited. I hear them chattering away about how much fun it will be when Lucy has her puppies. I'm excited too just thinking about having more babies around. They're so much fun. Lucy, of course, is clueless. It's way too early for her to know that she's pregnant.

Now that everything's settled with Lucy, my Pals start planning for the drive up to Wisconsin. It seems like everything's going well. We *have* done this before, you know. But I have noticed that, like me, my Pals are slowing down. It seems like Don is always going to see his doctor about something. Nobody seems to know what his problem is and I can tell he's not very happy about all this. My Pal always likes to do what he wants when he wants to do it. And now I think Patricia has a problem too. I hear my Pals talking about something called a "pacemaker." I've never heard about this thing before so I listen real hard. I think it's something they put inside you and hook up to your heart to make sure it keeps working. This seems like a good idea. I know that if I run around too fast and then stop, I'm panting and I can feel my heart going "thump, thump, thump." Then I really have to take some time to catch my breath. I wonder if they make pacemakers for dogs?

My Pals spend the rest of April getting ready for the drive up north. Sometime in early May, I hear my Pals planning for Patricia to go to the hospital to get her pacemaker put in. I'm always a little nervous whenever one of my Pals goes to the hospital. But Patricia is only gone one night. When she comes back we all rush over to jump on her and lick her, especially Lucy. Then Don says, "Okay, guys. Just take it easy. Let Patricia sit down." And we do.

I've figured out that everything went well but Patricia really does have to take it easy. I'm starting to think the drive up north will just be too hard on my Pals this year. Maybe we won't go up to the cabin now. Maybe Lucy will have her babies right here in Texas.

But guess what? Don's son Dan, who lives in Madison, comes up with an idea. He decides to charter a jet airplane for the trip. When I first hear about this, I'm a little worried because I'm remembering the times I had to be in a carrier in the baggage part of the airplane. I hated that so much. I guess Don must have seen me worrying and here's what he said: "Sally, you don't have to be afraid. This is a special plane just for us. We'll all be together." I'm so happy. Our very own plane! We won't have to go through all that waiting-in-line stuff at the airport. But—best of all—no carriers. Dan will fly down in the jet to get us and we'll all fly back to Madison, Wisconsin, together. And when we get there, Dan's going to lend us his Jeep to use for the summer.

22

Up, Up and Away!

My Pals are real busy for most of May getting ready for our plane trip north. I know it's getting close when they start carrying our luggage and all the other stuff we're taking out to the garage where the SUV is parked. Late next morning, I know we're almost ready to go when Misti comes over. She takes us out to do our business. When we're finished, our Pals are waiting. "Okay, let's go," they say, and we're off on another adventure.

We all pile into the SUV and Misti drives us over to the Lone Star Airport, which isn't very far from our house. No traveling all the way to Houston like we did when we went to New York and then to England.

Before we know it, we're there. Dan's jet has already landed and he comes over to the car and helps us carry our stuff onto the plane. Of course, we dogs are on our leashes when we walk up the steps to the plane. When we get inside, the pilot is there to greet us. He's a nice young guy. I hear him say this is the first time he's flown this plane. I don't want to think about *that* too much. He's very friendly to me and Cowboy and tells us to just look around for a good seat. But it's easy to see that, right from the start, our pilot just falls in love with Lucy. Well, that's not hard to do!

Once we're inside this plane, guess what? No leashes. Yippee! We can walk around wherever we want. And there's plenty of room to lie down on the floor or on one of the seats. After checking everything out, I pick my very own seat next to a window. Cowboy heads toward the back to pick out his own window seat. Lucy is still walking up and down the aisle checking everything out. She seems a little restless these days. I think she knows there's something going on inside her belly.

Pretty soon, I can hear some noise that I know from experience is the plane's engines. Then we hear the pilot's voice telling us to sit down and buckle our seat belts. Well, I can't buckle up, but I do sit down in my seat. Patricia calls Lucy over and she jumps up on the seat next to her. The plane is moving now and I can feel it starting to roll along faster and faster. Then, just like magic, we're up in the sky. I can see the clouds outside my very own window.

As soon as the pilot says we can unbuckle our seat belts, Lucy jumps off her seat and strolls up front. She sits down next to our pilot, who's now her new best friend. I think she might even be helping him fly the plane.

Me, I'm just "chilling out" in this nice soft seat. Then, I really do start feeling a little cold. Dan and Don are sitting across the aisle from me and I hear Dan say that private planes have to fly at 45,000 feet. He says that's 15,000 feet above the commercial airlines. That explains it. Even I know that—whether it's on a mountain or in a plane—the higher you get the colder you get. All I can do is curl up and snuggle against the back of my seat. I even manage to nap a little. When I wake up, I can't even see out my window. It's all frosted up. Patricia is sleeping and Don and Dan are talking business. So now I'm cold *and* bored. Then I hear Don say he's worried the plane might get hit by some screws and bolts or other space garbage. I'm not sure what he's talking about, but it doesn't sound good. Now I'm not bored anymore. I'm nervous. And a little scared. I just want to get where we're going. Cowboy wanders down the aisle and he doesn't seem bothered at all. Do you think we worry about things more as we get older?

The pilot told us at the beginning of the flight that it would take about two and a half hours to get to Madison. Finally, I can feel the plane going down and pretty soon, there's a little bounce. I think it's the wheels hitting the runway. Now the plane is slowing down. Finally, it stops. Thank goodness, we're here.

We've landed at a small, private airport outside Madison. My Pals put our leashes on and we head to the door of the plane. Of course, Licky Lucy has to stop and say goodbye to our pilot. He gives her a nice ear scratch before she goes. As we walk down the steps of the plane, we see Dan's wife Patti waving at us. We load all our stuff into their SUV and jump in. It's pretty crowded, but it's just a short drive to Dan's office where the red Jeep Cherokee we'll be using for the summer is parked. Once we get there, we have to unload everything and then load up again. Finally we're ready to head to the cabin. It will take us about two hours to get there, so my Pals want to leave right away. They want to get there before dark so we can see what we're doing when we unload all our stuff again.

It's a pretty easy trip. Patricia is driving. Don's sitting next to her. I'm in the back seat with Lucy and Cowboy. Of course, each of them has staked out a window seat. So I settle down in the middle and before I know it, I'm having a nice little nap. When I wake up, we're heading up Coon Lake Road to the cabin. That was easy!

It doesn't take us long to get the car unloaded and put all our stuff away. We've done this so many times. Before dinner, Patricia wants to get the nursery area all ready so Lucy can get used to it. She sets up the whelping bed in the hallway off the living room. It's quieter there. Patricia thinks the pups will feel more secure and Lucy will be able to tend to her babies better. We're all getting pretty excited about the birth of the pups. We're still not sure how many there will be. Back in Texas, Lucy had an ultrasound. It looked like there might be four babies, but it was pretty hard to tell. All we know is that we'll love them all, no matter how many there are. And we're grateful that Lucy hasn't had any problems with her pregnancy so far. Now we're just keeping our fingers and paws crossed.

The next morning, right after we have breakfast and do our business, Don says we're going to Minocqua to see the vet, Dr. Dunn. He's the one who's going to deliver Lucy's pups. I trust him a lot. He took real good care of me when I was sick. This time, he just wants to take a look at Lucy to make sure everything's going okay. When we get there, Patricia takes Lucy into the doc's office while Don, Cowboy and I sit in the waiting room. After a while Patricia and Lucy come out with Dr. Dunn. He took another ultrasound and he says there are only two babies. He says one of them is quite small and he's a little worried about that.

Before we leave, my Pals set up Lucy's delivery date. It will be Friday, June 1, only about a week away. I can hardly wait. Cowboy couldn't care less. Lucy seems happy just to be leaving the vet's office.

23

Hard Times

Over the next week, I can tell my Pals are kind of anxious. Lucy seems fine. She's had no problems with her pregnancy so far. Cowboy, of course, never worries about anything except getting fed on time. Finally, the big day is here. On Friday morning, we get up early to take Lucy to the vet. My Pals have decided to take me along to keep Lucy—or maybe *them*—company. Cowboy, however, will stay at home. After breakfast, the three of us dogs go out to do our business while Don and Patricia put the bedding in the Jeep for Lucy and her pups to lie on when we bring them back to the cabin.

At last, we're ready. My Pals open the door to the veranda so Cowboy doesn't get too bored. Then the rest of us climb into the Jeep. The vet wants Lucy in early so he can watch her for a while before doing the C-section. Then he wants to keep her and the babies for at least an hour after the delivery to make sure everyone is doing okay. Sometimes with a C-section delivery, he tells us, the mother doesn't always recognize the babies as her own. He wants to keep an eye on Lucy and her babies until he's sure they've bonded. I can't believe Lucy would have that kind of problem. She's such a loving little girl. Before Dr. Dunn takes Lucy away, my Pals give her kisses and pats and tell her everything is going to be okay. I give my girl one last lick. And then she's gone.

Don, Patricia, and I get back in the Jeep and drive into town to get something to eat. Then we just walk around until it's time to go back to the vet. It seems like forever until Dr. Dunn comes out. He tells us that Lucy has two little girls. He says he's put the smaller baby in a warming box and wants to keep her there a little longer. So we just sit and wait until the vet says it's okay to take Lucy and her babies home. My Pals put me in the Jeep first. Then Don carries Lucy and Patricia carries the two babies wrapped in a blanket out to the car and we head home.

Of course, when we get back to the cabin, Cowboy charges over to see us the minute we walk in the door. Don takes him out on the veranda and closes the door so we can settle Lucy and her babies down. Patricia puts Lucy and her two little girls in the whelping bed and sets up a heat lamp nearby to make sure the babies stay warm. But right away, there's a problem. Lucy doesn't want to stay in the bed. She keeps trying to pick up one or the other of the two babies in her mouth and take it somewhere else. Each time she does this, Patricia gently takes the pup from her and puts the little one back in the whelping bed. This goes on for a while. It seems like Lucy knows something's not right. She's trying to fix it.

After a little while, Lucy settles down in the whelping bed so her babies can nurse. But there's another problem. They don't seem to know what to do. Maybe it's because they were born a little early. Patricia is trying to help them start to nurse. She puts each pup on one of Lucy's teats so they'll get the idea. During all this, Patricia is talking quietly to Lucy, stroking her and the babies and telling Lucy not to worry. She's going through it all with my little girl.

I have to take a short break from watching Patricia, Lucy and her babies. I go into the living room to see how my other Pal is doing. Don's sitting at the table using his computer. I rub up against his leg to let him know I'm here and he reaches down and scratches behind my ears.

"I'm e-mailing everyone to let them know how things are going with Lucy's babies," he says. "We'll just have to wait and see, won't we Sally."

Patricia stays with Lucy and her babies all night. Sometime during the night, the smaller one dies. The vet had warned us that this one might not make it, but that doesn't make us feel any better. In the morning, I follow Patricia outside and watch her bury the little dead baby near our woodpile. She puts a stick in the ground so we'll know where the little one is.

The larger baby seems to be struggling too. Lucy is doing her best to get the baby to nurse. Later in the day, Patricia takes the baby and Lucy into one of the bedrooms that has bunk beds. She stretches out on the lower bunk with Lucy and the baby so she can help them as much as possible but still get a little sleep. I'm at the door of the room, watching and dozing. There's not much else I can do. Don finally goes to bed, but Patricia and Lucy keep trying to help the baby nurse. Lucy's getting frantic now. It's like she knows this is her last chance. She just keeps licking and licking her baby.

I must have fallen asleep. But sometime during the night, something wakes me up. Patricia is carrying the puppy and Lucy is right behind her. I follow them into the living room. Patricia stretches out on the sofa and puts the baby on her chest. Lucy jumps up and settles right next to Patricia and the baby—as close as she can get. Patricia is crying and Lucy is making sad little noises so I know she's crying too. I feel so bad because there's nothing I can do. I just watch and listen.

All through the night, Lucy never gives up. She just keeps licking her baby. After a while, Patricia puts the baby on Lucy's teat one more time. The baby tries to pull at the teat and then she just dies. I think it's about three o'clock in the morning. Patricia lets Lucy stay with her dead baby for the rest of the night. As usual, Don gets up pretty early and comes into the living room. Patricia has to tell him that the second baby died. My Pal's real upset too. Later this morning, Patricia wraps up Lucy's second baby and we go out and bury her next to the first one.

Lucy cries a lot during these first few days after she's lost her babies. She keeps going over to the sofa and rubbing it. Then she gives a little cry. I think she remembers that's where her last baby died. She probably still smells her baby too.

MY LITTLE GIRL SEEMS to be slowly getting over the loss of her babies. And my Pals are too. After a week or so, Lucy shows some interest in going outside. Now, when Patricia takes me and Cowboy out to play, Lucy comes along too. Don always used to come outside and watch us play. Now he never comes out. I've stopped worrying about Lucy. Now I'm worried about my Pal. He just seems to be getting weaker and weaker. Maybe it's because he isn't eating very much. And I can tell he's in a lot of pain just by the way he moves.

My Pal goes to see a doctor here in Rhinelander, but nothing seems to work. Patricia is making him nice things to eat and she does whatever she can to make him comfortable. I guess we're all kind of use to this. For the last few years my Pal has been having problems. Patricia would rush him to the doctor or the hospital and he would always recover. It makes me feel so sad when I see my Pal in pain because I can't do anything to help. All I can do is stay close to him so he knows I would help if I could. Don says if the pain doesn't get better, we'll all just have to go back home to Texas so he can go see his regular doctors.

All of us are taking it real easy this summer. We just want Lucy and Don to feel better. But one day in August, Don starts having trouble breathing. Patricia knows right away that something's really wrong. She calls the 911 number and says her husband is having an "attack" and we need help. Pretty soon we hear a siren and the emergency people drive up to the cabin. Patricia lets the two men in and they go over to talk to Don. They're talking quietly, asking him questions, trying to get him to relax. They don't seem to know what's going on with him and neither does Patricia. But then Patricia says she can see his heart muscle moving in his chest. She tells the EMS men that she thinks Don might be having a heart attack. She tells them that he might have had a couple of smaller heart attacks earlier in the summer. I didn't know anything about that.

Of course, I'm scared. And I can tell that Cowboy and Lucy are worried too. The three of us just go back and forth between all the people in the room. We want to help, but we don't know what to do. I guess we're getting in the way because after a while, Patricia takes the three of us out to the veranda and slides the glass door closed. All we can do now is stand there with our noses pressed against the glass and try to figure out what's happening inside.

Finally, the EMS guys get a stretcher, put my Pal on it, and take him out to the ambulance. Patricia is right beside Don telling him everything is going to be all right. They put my Pal in the back of the ambulance. One EMS guy gets in with him and the other one gets behind the wheel and they drive away. Patricia just stands there for a minute. Then she comes into the cabin and lets us back in from the

146

veranda. Then she goes into the bedroom and changes her clothes. When she comes out, she tells us that everything's going to be okay and that she'll be back soon. Then she goes out the door, locks it behind her and gets into the Jeep. We watch her drive away.

We don't know what to do. I try to stay calm so Lucy and Cowboy won't get upset. For a while it works but as time goes by we all get restless. We would like to go out and do our business but no one is here to open the door. We would like to know what's wrong with our Pal Don. We want Patricia to come back and tell us what's happening. Tell us everything is going to be okay.

It seems like forever, but at last we hear a car coming. We run to the door to see who's there and it's Patricia! We're all running around her, jumping on her, chirping like crazy. We're so glad she's home. Patricia tries to calm us down but we can tell she's worried, that things aren't right. We dogs just know.

The three of us follow Patricia into the bedroom. We watch as she pulls out a suitcase and starts throwing clothes in it. But she's so upset that she just starts grabbing things and carrying them outside and throwing them in the back of the Jeep. She gives us some dog food and while we're eating, she makes a phone call. I hear her say the name "Laurie," so I think she must be talking to the lady who comes to the cabin to clean. Patricia says, "Can you come over?" But I know it's not cleaning day. And anyway, it's too late to be cleaning.

After she turns off her cell phone, Patricia looks down at me, Cowboy, and Lucy and says, "I have to go be with Don, so Laurie's coming over to take care of you. I'll be back as soon as I can. Everything's going to be all right." But while she's saying this, she's kind of crying, so I don't think everything's going to be all right. Then she bends down and pats each of us on the head. Then she goes out the door and gets in the Jeep and drives off.

The three of us dogs just stand there looking out the window. We don't know what to think. We pace around the cabin for a little while and look out all the windows. But when we don't see anything, we lie down and just wait. I don't know how much time goes by, but suddenly my ears perk up. I think I hear a car coming up the driveway. Lucy and Cowboy hear it too. Our Pal is back! We all start running around the living room chirping like crazy. But when we go to the window we can see that the car isn't our red Jeep. Then a woman gets out and we can see that it's Laurie.

Even though she's not our Pal, when Laurie opens the cabin door, we all rush over to say hello. Maybe she's taking us to be with Patricia and Don. She talks to us quietly for a few minutes. Then she goes to the closet, gets our leashes, and clips them on our collars. Now we're really sure we'll be seeing our Pals soon. We don't want to be alone in the cabin anymore, so we're happy to go with Laurie. She lets us do our business first. Then we get in the back seat of her car and we're off. But I don't know where.

All the time she's driving, Laurie is talking to us. Saying she's sorry she can't take care of us while Patricia's gone. Saying everything will be okay. (I've heard that before.) Saying we have to go to the kennel in Rhinelander, but just for a little while. I'm worried about that word "kennel." Does she mean we have to get boxed up like we did to fly to New York or Europe. I don't know if I can do that again.

All during the ride the three of us dogs can't settle down. We have our noses pressed up against the side windows and we walk back and forth on the seat. Things outside look familiar. It does seem like we're headed for Rhinelander. After about twenty minutes, sure enough, we're in town. We've all been here before, so I think maybe we'll be meeting up with our Pals. But now Laurie is turning into a driveway. I know where we are and I don't like it one bit. I can see the sign for the kennel where Patricia takes us once a month to get a shampoo and our nails clipped. That's no fun at all. And one time, my Pals left Lucy and me here overnight because they had to go somewhere. Now Laurie's pulling into the parking lot. "Here we are, gang," she says. "They're going to take good care of you until your Mom comes back to get you." Laurie gets out, opens the back door of the car, grabs our leashes, and we all head toward the building. Once we're inside, she tells the woman at the desk that we're the "Rashke dogs." The woman says, "Oh yes, we've been expecting you. I'll get someone to take them back."

Laurie walks us over to some chairs and she sits down. Lucy, Cowboy and I sit on the floor and wait to see what's going to happen next. What else can we do? Before long a young man comes through an inside door and walks over to us. He speaks quietly and holds out his hand a little and doesn't seem to mind when we start sniffing him.

I can smell other dogs on him. After a little more sniffing, he takes our leashes from Laurie and says, "Okay, guys, let's go." Laurie pats our heads one more time, gets up, and walks out the front door.

The young man walks us through the other door and down a hallway. He's talking quietly to us all the time and saying his name is Eric and that he'll take good care of us. He leads us into the big room where the kennels are. There are dogs in some of them who start to bark a little when they see us. Eric talks to them and they quiet down. Then he takes us over to the other side of the room, a little bit away from the other dogs. There are two kennels—a regular size one and a large one. Eric leads us over to the smaller one, opens the door, and Cowboy walks right in. He's so used to being in a kennel that he thinks nothing of it. Then Eric leads Lucy and me to the larger kennel and says, "Okay, girls, you two can share this one." I think that's really nice of him to let me and Lucy stay together. I want to keep a close eye on my little girl. She's had a hard time. I walk into the kennel and Lucy is happy to follow right behind.

After talking to us some more in his nice quiet voice, Eric leaves. I'm glad to see there's a bowl of water in the kennel. I'm pretty thirsty by now. I'm also starting to get hungry and I think Lucy and Cowboy are too. I wonder what time they serve dinner around here? There's not much the three of us can do now but lie down and wait and see what happens next and hope our Pals don't forget about us and leave us here forever. What will we do without them?

24

Waiting for Our Pals

I think we've been in this kennel about a week now. I'm not sure because every day is pretty much the same. All of us dogs wake up early—as soon as some light starts to come through the windows. Lucy and I usually stay curled up next to each other until one of the staff people comes in. There's nothing much to do when you're just sitting in the kennel waiting. When someone finally comes, they let us out of our cages, put our leashes on and take us outside to the open-air run in the back. Then, we're off our leashes to do our business and get some fresh air and exercise. It's a pretty big space and it feels real good to be out of the kennel. It's funny how just a little fresh air and space to run—slowly in my case—can mean so much. But our life is different now and I'm learning to be grateful for whatever I get.

After about half an hour, we go back into our kennels where our breakfast and fresh water is waiting. The rest of the day we spend either in the kennel or out in the backyard. Staff people come in to check on us. I like it most when Eric comes. He always talks to us and will open the kennel door to give us pats and scratches. It's nice, for sure, but it's not like home.

Today, sometime in the afternoon after we've come in from the run, Eric walks into the kennel area smiling. He comes over to our kennels and starts talking to Cowboy, Lucy and me. We've been napping, but our ears perk up when he says, "Okay, you lucky guys, it's time to go." Go where? We just got back from our exercise. I'm wondering what's up but Eric already has Cowboy out of his kennel and is putting the leash on. Now he puts the leashes on Lucy and me. We're all looking up at him, wondering what's next. Eric takes us out the door of the kennel area, but instead of leading us outside to the run again, he walks us down the hallway, opens the door to the waiting area, and takes us through.

Oh my! There she is—our Pal Patricia. She's bending down and holding out her hands. Eric is smart enough to drop our leashes so we can run over to our Pal. The three of us are chirping, wagging our tails, licking Patricia and running all around her. Patricia's crying now and saying how much she missed us and that everything is going to be all right and we're going home. We're so excited to see our Pal that we don't even notice there's another woman standing next to her smiling. When things finally settle down a bit, I can see that it's Patricia's daughter, Theresa. I guess she's come to help out her mom.

Theresa holds our leashes while Patricia goes over to the desk to pay our bill. When she finishes, we all head out the door. There's the Jeep in the parking space and we get in—us dogs in the back, Patricia driving, and Theresa next to her. On the way back to the cabin, we stop at a grocery store to get some food. Patricia and Theresa leave us in the car but they say they'll be right back. Well, not soon enough, I'm afraid. When they do get back, Patricia opens the Jeep's rear door to put the packages in and I hear her say, "What's that nasty smell?" We dogs know what it is and Patricia soon finds out. While she was in the store with Theresa, Cowboy was leaving her a gift on a blanket in the back seat—a huge pile of dog shit. It's like he had saved it all up just for her. I'm sure Patricia is going to be furious and give Cowboy hell. He looks guilty as all get out and he won't even look at his Pal.

But Patricia doesn't get mad. She just sighs and says, "Oh, Cowboy, you've never done anything like this before. I know you're mad at us, but we're not going away any more." Then she and Theresa ball up the blanket of shit and throw it in a nearby dumpster.

When we get back to the cabin, Patricia and Theresa start packing up a lot of things. Then they load them in the Jeep. Lucy and Cowboy and I are standing around watching all this and trying to figure out what's going on. I'm afraid they're going to leave us again. But then, just as the Jeep looks like it can't hold any more stuff, Patricia comes back into the cabin and says, "Let's go for a ride to the post office." Although we can't go into the post office, we watch

151

Patricia and Theresa carry in the packages to send back to Houston. We do this same thing together a few more times until, finally, there isn't anything left to send home.

Then Patricia and Theresa get us all packed up and say we're going to see our Pal Don in Madison. When we get to Madison, we check in at the Marriott Hotel. Misti is already there. I think she came on the plane with Theresa. But she stayed here in Madison to look after my Pal while Patricia and Theresa came to get us dogs in Rhinelander.

The next day, Patricia picks up my leash and says, "Come on, Sally, let's go see Don." Patricia and I and Misti and Theresa all get in the Jeep. We drive for a while. Then we stop at a big building that Patricia says is the hospital where my Pal is staying. After we park, Misti takes my leash and the four of us go into this hospital building. Patricia leans over and pats my head. She says that she and Theresa are going upstairs now to get my Pal. Misti leads me over to another door and we walk through. We're outside again on this beautiful patio with lots of flowers and other plants. It's very peaceful. Misti says this is the Pavilion where you can visit with the patients in the hospital.

I'm looking all around this nice place. Then I see Theresa pushing a wheelchair. Patricia's walking alongside. As soon as I see who's in the wheelchair, I start chirping. It's my Pal! I'm pulling really hard on my leash now. Finally Misti just lets it go. I run over to see Don. He looks very tired, but I can tell he is happy to see me. I get as close as I can to his wheelchair. Then my Pal puts his arm over the side of the chair and I stand up on my back legs and put my head under his arm. We just stay like that until Patricia bends over and tells me I have to get down because my Pal needs to rest. On our way back to the hotel, Patricia tells me we'll all be going home in a few days. Thank goodness. I can't wait.

A couple of days later, we pick up my Pal at the hospital and drive to the airport. Misti has already gone home but Theresa is flying back with Don and Patricia and us dogs. Lucy, Cowboy and I watch as Don's sons, Dan and Bruce, help him walk up the stairs to the plane. All of a sudden Don slips and falls and scrapes his leg. Dan and Bruce help him up and hold onto his arms as they go the rest of the way up the stairs. Then Patricia and Theresa and Cowboy and

Lucy and I go up the stairs too. Inside the plane someone is putting a bandage on my Pal's leg. When Don is settled in his plane seat, I jump up and sit next to him. I stay there for the whole trip, except for a few times while he's sleeping. Then I get down and stretch my legs a little. Lucy and Cowboy are hanging out most of the time in the back of the plane. We are all so tired.

25

Home Is Where the Heart Is

After a couple of hours in the air, we land at Lone Star Airport. It seems like such a long time since we took off from here. But I think it's only been about two months. Lucy, Cowboy and I are so happy to be here because we are pretty sure we're going home. At least, that's what Patricia says. And Don shakes his head "yes" too.

Patricia's niece, Cheryl, and her husband are at the airport to meet us and take my Pals home. And Misti has come in her own car to take us dogs and the luggage home too. She comes up the stairs to the plane, clips our leashes on, and says, "Don't worry. We're all going home." When we reach the bottom of the stairs, we all turn around and watch as Patricia's niece holds onto Don's arm and helps him down the stairs. Patricia is right behind them. I'm so glad when my Pal makes it to the bottom. Thank goodness the car is parked close by so Don doesn't have to walk very far.

It doesn't take us long to drive home. The first thing Patricia does is help my Pal into the house. She says he should go lie down in the bedroom for a while. For once, Don doesn't argue with her. The next few days, my Pal spends a lot of time resting. I'm always happy when he comes into the living room. We can just sit together and be quiet. Before Don got sick, I always used to sit in his lap. Now, he can't hold me anymore. What he does is hang his arm over the side of the sofa or the chair where he's sitting. And I just put myself under his hand like I did at the hospital in Madison. My Pal starts rubbing me and scratching behind my ears and it feels so good. I think it makes him feel good too. Some days, when he's feeling a little stronger, he'll walk around the living room with his "walker." That's what my Pal calls it. It's a metal thing that he can hold onto with both hands so he doesn't have to worry about falling. He walks real slow. And I walk real slow right behind him. It's my job now to take care of him and make sure he doesn't get hurt.

My Pal and I just like to sit together quietly now.

One day, I hear Patricia and Don talking. She says she thinks he might have a bladder infection. She wants to take him to the local hospital to have a checkup. Don doesn't want to go but Patricia finally convinces him. I guess he figures she will just keep nagging until he says yes. And he's right.

When my Pals get back from the hospital, I hear Patricia talking to one of her daughters on the phone. She says the doctors can't find anything wrong with his bladder. For the next two days, I can tell that my Pal still isn't feeling any better. But he won't even talk to

Patricia about going to see his doctors in Houston. He says he wants to stay home and watch the Sunday football game on TV. Like me, Patricia knows how stubborn my Pal can be. So she just stops talking about Houston.

When Sunday comes around, Don, Patricia, me, Lucy, and Cowboy all gather in the living room to watch the game. But by halftime, Don is so tired that he has to go back to bed. I know how much he loves his football games, so he must feel really bad if he can only watch half of the game.

The next morning, I'm in the bedroom just spending time with my Pal, who's still in bed resting. Patricia comes into the room and climbs on the bed. As they're sitting there together, Don says he knows he has to go to the hospital in Houston. Right away, Patricia starts making a bunch of phone calls. The next day, our dog sitter Tolef comes and Don and Patricia leave. It seems like many days go by. Tolef is taking good care of us like he always does. But I'm worrying all the time about my Pal. When is he coming back? Then, one day—it's Sunday, I think—Don and Patricia come home. I know everything will be okay now that we're all back together again.

But it doesn't take me long to see that everything is not okay. His first night home, Don sleeps in the recliner in his office. He's never done that before. And something is wrong with Patricia. She just lies on the "white sofa" where none of us dogs are allowed to sit. She looks like she's been crying. I go over and lick her hand and she starts crying again. Two of her "girls"—Misti and Theresa—are also here now. It doesn't look like they're going to leave any time soon. I think I heard them say that Patricia's other daughter, Stephanie, is coming on Thursday. What's going on? Don't they know I can take care of my Pal? But no one listens to me. And now they won't even let me go into the bedroom to see Don.

Finally, Patricia gets up from the white sofa. On Monday things really start happening. The girls are moving stuff all over the place. The pool table goes out of the Trophy Room and other things go in. A strange looking bed arrives and that goes in the Trophy Room too. A lot of people I don't know come and go. I hear someone say "hospice." During all of this, I see Patricia crying again. I know it must have something to do with my Pal. I haven't seen him since he got back from the hospital.

I finally see my Pal in the evening. Misti brings him into the living room. He's in a wheelchair again. Everyone settles down to see my Pals' favorite TV show. It's called "The Voice." We're all watching the show together and everyone seems happy. Patricia and Misti and Theresa are singing and dancing all around the living room. But I'm watching my Pal Don. He looks sick and very tired, but he's smiling. Maybe everything will be okay after all.

When the show is over, the girls wheel Don into the Trophy Room. Now I understand. They were fixing up a special room for my Pal. That's what the funny looking bed was for. You can make it go up or down so my Pal can rest easier. Patricia is crying again. Misti tells her mother to go on to bed. She says she'll watch over Don that night. Patricia calls Lucy and Cowboy and they follow her to the bedroom where they have their beds too. Misti brings my bed into the Trophy Room and puts it on the floor next to Don's funny bed. So now we can both look after him. Misti was the first person I loved when I came to America. She's also my Pal's adopted daughter and she loves him very much. But not as much as I do. I'm staying right here all the time and I'm not going to let anyone upset my Pal. I'll take care of him and I'll only leave for a few minutes when I have to go outside to do my business.

The Trophy Room is nice and bright. My Pal's bed faces the windows that look out over the swimming pool in our backyard. We have a routine now. Theresa comes in and gives my Pal his medicine at different times during the day. And every night Misti sleeps in a chair in Don's room. She sets the alarm on her cell phone to ring every hour so she can get up and check on him. But I would be the first to know if anything bad was happening. I sleep on the bed at night right next to my Pal. Misti helps me get up there because I can't jump as good as I used to. I also watch out for my Pal during the day. Sometimes Patricia comes in and starts fussing around to make sure Don is comfortable. I can see it's just too much for him. That's when I have to growl at Patricia a little. When I do, she stops all the fussing and just sits with Don and holds his hand.

ON TUESDAY AFTERNOON, my Pal's brother Richard arrives. Don has been waiting for him. Even though my Pal is a little groggy from all the medicine he has to take, he and Richard talk for a long time. I just sit in my bed and listen to them. In the evening, Patricia and Theresa wheel Don out to the living room again so we can all watch another TV show that Don really likes—"Dancing with the Stars."

On Wednesday, Richard spends a lot of time in Don's room. I stay in my bed and listen. They're talking about old times and laughing a lot. It makes me think of when we were all together up at the cabin in Wisconsin. Sometimes, I don't understand what they're saying. Richard asks Don: "What do you think is going to happen to you after you die?" Don says: "I have no idea."

Don tells Richard he wants his ashes scattered on Lake Mildred. My ears perk up. That's the lake by our cabin. I don't know what these "ashes" are. But I feel better when Richard says, "Don't worry. I'll be there." Then he asks Don, "What do you want to come back as—a large mouth or a small mouth bass?" When my Pal hears this, he starts laughing so hard and I get really scared. But finally, he calms down. Then he and Richard just sit talking quietly. Things are okay now, I think. I can take a little nap.

When I wake up I hear Don tell Richard he wants to talk with his kids. Richard says he'll set it up and he doesn't waste any time. He calls Don's son Bruce and asks him to contact his other brothers and sisters. My Pal tells Misti he's not going to take his morphine medicine for a while because he wants to be alert when his kids call. One by one, Don's children call their dad. After the last call, my Pal takes his morphine. He seems very sad. He says to Richard: "I had so much to say to them and so little time to say it." Misti says she's going to give him his anti-depressant pill. I hope that makes him not so sad.

On Thursday morning I wake up real early. I'm surprised to see that Don is awake too. I just sit there on the bed for a while with my Pal. He seems a little restless and he keeps looking at the clock. Then he reaches over to the table next to his bed and picks up a framed picture of Patricia that he keeps there. He just lies in bed holding that picture and looking at it. I try to be real quiet when I jump down from the bed so I don't disturb him. I feel kind of strange but I can't figure out what's wrong. Misti is already up and she brings me my breakfast as usual. Then I take a little nap in my bed on the floor.

I wake up when I hear someone come into the room. It's Richard. He and my Pal are talking quietly now. Richard says he'll be leaving soon for the airport to go back home to Washington. Then Richard says, "Well, Bro, when we meet at the Pearly Gates, I'll have my saxophone ready. What do you want me to play?" Don doesn't say anything for a minute. I guess he's thinking. Then he says, "When the Saints Go Marching In." "You got it," Richard says. Then he leans over and gives my Pal a hug.

"Goodbye, Bro," Richard says.

When Richard leaves the room, I follow him. I need to stretch my legs a little. He goes down the hall to my Pal's office. He walks in, sits in the chair, and puts his head down on Don's desk. I think he needs to be alone. And I need to be with my Pal. I leave Richard and go back to the Trophy Room.

A little later, I hear Patricia come in. She asks Misti to help her fix her hair and makeup. When Patricia comes back, she's wearing a beautiful dress and a necklace that Don gave her. And, of course, my nose tells me she's wearing the perfume Don really likes. Patricia spends most of the day just sitting in the chair next to Don's bed and holding his hand. When she needs to leave the room to cry, my Pal holds her picture until she comes back.

LATE IN THE AFTERNOON, while Patricia is taking a little break, her daughter Stephanie comes in and sits down in the chair next to my Pal's bed. The two of them are talking quietly and I'm just starting to doze off when I hear Don say the word "heaven." I don't think I've ever heard my Pal say anything about heaven before. But now he and Stephanie are talking about how "beautiful" and "glorious" heaven must be. They talk a little more about what this heaven place is like. Then Stephanie says she's going to get Patricia. I follow her down the hall and stand outside the master bedroom. That's when I hear Stephanie say to Patricia: "Mom, I think you need to come and sit with your husband." When I hear that, I just turn right around. I know I have to go sit with my Pal too.

Patricia comes into the Trophy Room right after me. "I've been waiting for you," Don says. "I want to tell you goodbye."

I don't understand what my Pal is talking about. Nobody's going anywhere. Patricia climbs onto the bed next to Don and Misti comes in to help me get up on the bed too. Then Misti leaves and it's so peaceful here with just the three of us. Patricia is crying a little and then she kisses Don and leaves red lipstick marks on his face. Now Don starts to groan. But it's not from the kisses. Patricia gets off the bed and says she's going to get the nitroglycerin. When she comes back, Don looks at her and says, "No more, honey. I am ready."

Oh no. What is happening?

Now everything is very quiet. I want someone to come and tell me everything will be okay. But I know my Pal has left me. And I know I have to leave this room because my Pal isn't here anymore. I walk slowly down the hall to the back door. I'm trying to chirp, but my voice cracks. I lie down on the floor alone. My heart is broken.

AFTER A WHILE, A MAN AND A WOMAN who are my Pals' friends come over to the house. They take Patricia out to the gazebo in the backyard. But I stay inside. Then some men come and I know they are taking my Pal's body away. Just like Patricia took away the bodies of Lucy's dead babies. I'm sitting on the floor in the living room when the man who took Patricia outside—I think his name is Milt—comes in and sits down on the sofa. He looks at me and holds out his hand, just like my Pal used to do. I walk over to the sofa, jump up, and put my chin on his leg like I did with my Pal. He strokes my head and back and we just sit there together for a long time. It helps a little.

A couple of days go by and Patricia tells me and Lucy and Cowboy that she has to go away for a few days. She says she's sorry to leave us right now, but she has to go to Don's funeral in Madison. I think that's where all the family will get together to say goodbye to my Pal. It would be too sad for me to go there.

Cheryl, Patricia's niece, is at the house now. She's helping Patricia dress and get ready to go to the airport. After Patricia leaves, Cheryl takes Cowboy, Lucy and me out to her car. She says we're driving over to Bed, Bath and Biscuit. That's where we go for grooming and sometimes for a short boarding stay. When we get to "The Biscuit," as everyone calls it, Cheryl says, "Sally, you stay here in the car. I'll only be a minute." Then she puts Cowboy and Lucy on their leashes and takes them inside.

When Cheryl comes back, she says, "Sally, your Mom knows how sad you are. She's worried about you and she wants you to stay with me while she's away. It won't be for very long." This makes me feel a little better. It's good to know that the only Pal I have left is thinking about me. Being sad at Cheryl's house is better than being sad at the kennel.

PATRICIA IS BACK NOW and we are all trying to learn to live without our Pal. But I'll never be the same. I'll never be as happy as I was. I know Patricia is sad too. But she is helping me as much as she can. She even goes out with me when I need to pee. Whenever I go outside now, I always sniff around. I'm still looking for my Pal.

Afterword

DONALD NORMAN RASHKE died on September 27, 2012. After the funeral service in Madison, I was given a shaker box containing some of Don's ashes. Don's son Dan was also given one.

That same day, I went with my family—my daughters Theresa and her husband Gorman, Misti and her husband Peter, Stephanie and her husband Jeff, and my granddaughter Jessica—up to the cabin. We headed to the lake where our boat was still moored at the pier. All of us climbed aboard and someone—I can't remember who—began a prayer. Then each person picked up from the one before until the prayer finally came to me. I said a few words. Then I held the box over the water and turned it upside down. We all watched Don's ashes fall into the lake. Then we left the boat and walked quietly to our cars. We headed back to Madison, each of us grieving in our own way. A few days after I got back home, I received an urn containing most of Don's ashes. Besides the Navy insignia honoring Don's naval service many years before, the urn was also engraved with the words "Honey, I love you. Patricia."

ON SATURDAY MORNING, May 25, 2013, Don's brother, Richard, and Don's son, Dan, drove from Madison up to Rhinelander where they met up as planned with Don's other kids who still lived in Wisconsin—Guy, Bruce, Richard (Richie), and Terri. They had brunch together in town. Then they headed over to Lake Mildred near the cabin where Don and I, the dogs, and visiting kids and grandkids had spent many happy summers.

Guy, Don's oldest son, had his motorboat in tow. It was a bright, sunny day with hardly any wind. The lake was calm and almost empty. Guy steered the boat toward the middle of the lake, then cut the engine.

Richard told the group about his conversation with Don shortly before he died. Then he started to sing. "Oh when the Saints… go marching in…" Don's kids joined in. "Oh when the Saints go marching in…I want to be among that number…when the Saints go marching in."

They sang an encore and then sat quietly while Guy opened the shaker box that Dan had brought and slowly sprinkled his father's ashes onto the lake. Everyone was silent for a few more minutes. Then they headed back to shore and everyone drove over to the cabin where a lot of small items—hats, dishes, pictures, books, some clothes—were laid out for anyone to take. Then everyone left and headed to Terri's farm outside Steven's Point for dinner and the trip home.

FOR SEVERAL DAYS AFTER DON'S DEATH, Sally followed me everywhere. Then she stopped and Lucy began to follow me. Sally seemed to be saying: I've helped my remaining Pal as much as I can. Now, Lucy, it's your turn to look after her. And then, for a while, Sally went on with her grieving—as we all did.

Sometime during the week after Don died, I got a call from the doctor in Madison who had performed the emergency surgery on Don. He was calling to offer his condolences. He said the nurse practitioner who worked with him had seen Don's obituary in the Madison paper and told him about it. The doctor told me he was sorry he hadn't been able to help Don very much. I said, "No, that's not true. You gave him a lot. You gave him two extra weeks. Those were so important to him."

Those last two weeks were important not just for Don, but for all of us—me, my daughters, Don's brother, Richard, and Don's children. And, of course, the dogs, especially Sally. At one point during Don's final days, I asked him about the book he and Sally were working on. Did he want us to finish it and make sure it was published? Don said yes and I promised him that Sally and I would see it through. Although those last two weeks were very hard and sad ones, I wouldn't trade them for anything. They gave all of us time just to be together in our home and show our love, each of us in our own way. Everyone should be so lucky.

AROUND THE ONE YEAR ANNIVERSARY of Don's death, my daughter (and Don's adopted daughter) Misti flew in from California. It was a difficult weekend for both of us. We waited until the day Misti was supposed to fly back to California to do what we had to do. In fact, we put it off until it was almost time for her to go to the airport. The rain was coming down hard and looked like it would never stop. We drove to the middle of the bridge that spans Lake Conroe, stopped the car, and got out in the pouring rain. Misti had the urn containing Don's ashes and I had a shaker box that we planned to use to sprinkle his ashes over the water as Don had asked. My daughter and I looked at each other and I said, "Just drop it." Her eyes widened briefly. Then she let go of the urn. We watched it fall downward, hit the water, and disappear.

I know it was selfishness on my part. Don didn't want his ashes to remain in the urn. But I wanted to hold onto him in some way just a little longer, to know that his remains were in one particular place. Misti and I stood on the bridge for a few more minutes and I wept for myself and for missing him so much and for Sally, his second love.

Patricia Rashke
April 2015

Acknowledgements

I WOULD LIKE TO THANK Grace Haynes for getting us started on this adventure; Roger Pugh for mentoring Don on breeding and showing the dogs; professional handler Michelle Aguillard, who took Cowboy from Champion to Grand Champion Silver; and the many other handlers and friends we made along the way. I would also like to thank Paula Kaufmann for her editorial help on this project.

PR

About the Author

SALLY'S PAL DON RASHKE helped her write *Adventures of Mustang Sally*. Before moving to Texas and marrying Patricia, Mr. Rashke was the founder and CEO of a successful employee benefits services company based in Wisconsin. With Sally's arrival, Don and his wife fell in love with Staffies. They started showing Sally, set up Mustang Sally's Kennel, and carefully bred her to preserve the best qualities of the breed in her pups. Sally and her babies won many ribbons in dog shows across the country.

Printed in the United States
By Bookmasters